DWELL
IN PEACE

Applying Nonviolence
to Everyday Relationships

DWELL IN PEACE

Applying Nonviolence to Everyday Relationships

Ronald C. Arnett

THE BRETHREN PRESS, Elgin, Illinois

DWELL IN PEACE

Cover Design by Ken Stanley

Library of Congress Cataloging in Publication Data

Arnett, Ronald C   1952-
    Dwell in peace.

    Bibliography: p.
    1. Nonviolence—Moral and religious aspects.
2. Peace. 3. Interpersonal relations. I. Title.
[BT736.6.A76]   261.8′3   79-24639
ISBN O-87178-199-9

Table of Contents

Foreword

Brethren have often appreciated the slogan of those who epitomize that there is no way to peace because peace is the way. Even though we have claimed our peace stance applies to all of life, we have too often relegated it to times when our offspring face military conscription. We have even judged our own faithfulness to our heritage by the way our eighteen year olds respond to a draft.

For this reason it is wonderful to have the contribution of one who has applied the gospel of peace helpfully and wisely to day by day ways of dealing with interpersonal conflict. It is a real tribute to Paul Keller and his long teaching ministry in the field of communications that students like Ronald Arnett creatively integrate their academic specialties with the peace heritage. Ron has done for the Brethren what so many Mennonites have done in their academic pilgrimages, namely, attempt to apply the best from the heritage to basic areas of research. The book reveals the author's rootage in the Brethren peace position as well as his acquaintance with the wider peace movement through frequent references to Gandhian methodology and Quaker Gene Sharp's research in nonviolent social strategy. At the same time the pacifist stance is brought in dialogue with some of the best contemporary insights from the fields of communication, psychology, and philosophy. One can find in the social sciences that which validates some of the best hunches in the Brethren style of peacemaking.

Recognizing the many ways we daily do violence to others, this book attempts to point to the nonviolent resolution of interpersonal conflicts. The author does not want to allow us to run away from conflict. Rather, we are to deal with it in ways which avoid violating persons. In this framework, he deals with images of good and evil and offers a balanced position which I feel is consistent with most Brethren views on the nature of a person. There is an excellent critique of current self-realization fads. A sound view of community emerges as the author rejects both self-centered individualism and oppressive collectivism. Radical commitment is not put aside for the sake of a superficial peace. Rather, one is to stand one's ground in a posture of caring confrontation which remains open to others. Such themes are clarified through excellent illustrations and buttressed by many quotes from great spirits such as Jewish philosopher and peacemaker, Martin Buber.

The Brethren Press is to be complimented for risking the publication of a quite substantial academic book. At the same time most folk will find it quite readable. It should circulate widely in Brethren circles, among those involved in the art of speech and communication, in peace and conflict academic programs, and among those interested in nonviolent peacemaking.

Dale W. Brown

Preface

I have been asked by my students, colleagues, and those who have read some of my works how a nonviolent peacemaking orientation became the foundation for my understanding of interpersonal communication and interpersonal conflict. Clearly, it is impossible for me to properly acknowledge all who contributed to the development of this viewpoint, because it is the result of an emotional and intellectual search that began in my high school years. However, I can point to an outline of experiences that reveal the beginning of my peacemaking stance.

I was significantly influenced by the Vietnam War. My high school and college years were intimately touched by the Vietnam experience. I lived with the daily knowledge of the horror of war. I did not have to be in Vietnam to witness the taking of human life; all I needed to do was to pick up a newspaper or watch the evening news to see such actions. The inhumanity of war and the fact that no one I talked to seemed to know why we were in Vietnam made me question our involvement. I became suspicious of slogans and cliches that were not based on reasoned rationales about our actions in Vietnam.

At Manchester College, my questioning opposition to the Vietnam War matured from association and sharing with the students, faculty, and friends I met. My opposition to the Vietnam War, which had begun in seeming isolation, was suddenly supported by an intellectual community. I witnessed individuals struggling to gain conscientious objector status and others going to jail as symbolic consciences of our nation. I met Rev. Carroll Petry, then the pastor at Eel River Church of the Brethren, who encouraged my active association with this historic peace church. With my Church of the Brethren involvement, I discovered a foundation for my opposition to war.

Two other important experiences broadened my understanding of the peace witness. First, my association with the Church of the Brethren Mission in Lybrook, New Mexico, exposed me to some dedicated individuals who were sensitive to the Navaho culture. They were acutely aware that the dominant white culture had systematically worked to destroy the indigenous cultures of American Indians. The fact that foreign cultures could oppress and violate different cultural viewpoints became blatantly clear to me. Second, my pastoral experience at Bethel Center Church of the Brethren allowed me to see committed people work to affirm others without violating their human dignity. My understanding of the peace witness now included the insight that human beings need not be physically abused to be violated. A foreign culture and insensitive people can violate others. At this point, I became convinced that nonviolent peacemaking was a necessary foundation for dealing with others, not only in war but in daily living.

In my graduate school studies in interpersonal communication at Ohio University, I was further able to root my learnings about peace in an intellectual framework. Dr. Ray Wagner, the chairperson of my master's and doctoral work, encouraged my intellectual pursuit of the connections between communication and nonviolent peacemaking. This book in its initial stages was read numerous times and critiqued by Dr. Wagner. Also, Dr. Paul Keller from Manchester College provided helpful input into the early work on this project. This book is the result of my dissertation work sponsored by Dr. Wagner, Dr. Keller and the rest of my Ph.D. committee and an additional two years of research and revision. Thus, I am grateful to the members of my doctoral committee for their support in that initial effort. Perhaps more significantly, Drs. Wagner and Keller provided a teaching model rooted in a peacemaking ethic that continues to influence my own teaching style.

Most importantly is the contribution of my wife, Millie. My commitment to peace has been supported and enriched by my association with her. Millie's commitment and life help to sustain my faith that a more peaceful world is a liveable possibility. The experiences related above have been given even greater depth and meaning, because we have lived through them together.

I have been fortunate to have people challenge me to move forward at crucial points in my life. This peacemaking style of caring confrontation called me to explore alternatives to violent approaches to conflict. Indeed, my world-view, like any, did not emerge out of an interpersonal vacuum. I have been and I am being shaped by significant people in my life. In recognition of this fact, this book is dedicated to the generations before and after mine — to my parents and my son, Adam Geoffrey, whose generation more than any other may have to seriously explore and implement the alternative of nonviolent peacemaking. My prayers and my hope are with them.

Ronald C. Arnett
St. Cloud, Minnesota
July, 1979

Acknowledgements

During the beginning groundwork for this book, I interviewed individuals associated with the three historic peace churches: Church of the Brethren, Quaker, and Mennonite. Their viewpoints and understandings about dealing with interpersonal conflict from a nonviolent peacemaking perspective pointed me in helpful directions. Some of their statements are used in this book and are set off appropriately as quotes. The quotations are not individually footnoted, in order for me to use them to exemplify points, without concern about misrepresenting a person's viewpoint. With thanks and appreciation, I have listed below the representatives of the historic peace churches and their locations, as of the interviews in the summer of 1976.

Baldwin, Ferne. Manchester College, North Manchester, Indiana.
Beechy, Atlee. Goshen College, Goshen, Indiana.
Bittinger, Desmond. San Diego, California.
Bittinger, Emmert F. Bridgewater College, Bridgewater, Virginia.
Black, Louise. Elizabethtown College, Elizabethtown, Pennsylvania.
Bowman, Warren D. Bridgewater, Virginia.
Brown, Dale. Bethany Theological Seminary, Oak Brook, Illinois.
Brown, Kenneth. Manchester College, North Manchester, Indiana.
Burkholder, J. Lawrence. Goshen College, Goshen, Indiana.
Burkholder, J. R. Goshen College, Goshen, Indiana.
Cassel, John. Bethany Theological Seminary, Oak Brook, Illinois.
Crill, Edward. Elizabethtown College, Elizabethtown, Pennsylvania.
Crist, Wayne. McPherson Church of the Brethren, McPherson, Kansas.
Deeter, Allen. Manchester College, North Manchester, Indiana.
Durnbaugh, Don. Bethany Theological Seminary, Oak Brook, Illinois.
Dyck, C. J. Associated Mennonite Biblical Seminaries, Elkhart, Indiana.
Eby, Horner. Lombard, Illinois.
Eiler, David. Manchester College, North Manchester, Indiana.
Eisenbise, Russell. Elizabethtown College, Elizabethtown, Pennsylvania.
Evans, T. Quentin. Manchester College, North Manchester, Indiana.

Fike, Oscar. Bridgewater, Virginia.
Greiner, Gerald. Elizabethtown College, Elizabethtown, Pennsylvania.
Hoffman, Paul. McPherson College, McPherson, Kansas.
Hoover, Wilbur. McPherson, Kansas.
Hoskins, Lewis. Earlham College, Richmond, Indiana.
Just, Roy. Tabor College, Hillsboro, Kansas.
Keim, Albert. Eastern Mennonite College, Harrisonburg, Virginia.
Keller, Paul. Manchester College, North Manchester, Indiana.
Knechel, Robert. Manchester College, North Manchester, Indiana.
Landrum, Richard. Stone Church of the Brethren, Huntingdon, Pennsylvania.
Lengel, Leland. McPherson College, McPherson, Kansas.
McFadden, Robert. Bridgewater College, Bridgewater, Virginia.
McMasters, Richard. James Madison University, Harrisonburg, Virginia.
Miller, Paul. McPherson College, McPherson, Kansas.
Mullen, Nancy. Earlham School of Religion, Richmond, Indiana.
Neher, Dean. Bridgewater College, Bridgewater, Virginia.
Puffenberger, William. Elizabethtown College, Elizabethtown, Pennsylvania.
Richards, Howard. Earlham College, Richmond, Indiana.
Rieman, T. Wayne. Manchester College, North Manchester, Indiana.
Roop, Eugene F. Earlham College, Richmond, Indiana.
Rushby, William F. Eastern Mennonite College, Harrisonburg, Virginia.
Schwartzentruber, Hubert. Mennonite Board of Congregational Ministries, Elkhart, Indiana.
Wagoner, Paul. McPherson College, McPherson, Kansas.
Zeigler, Carl. Elizabethtown College, Elizabethtown, Pennsylvania.
Zigler, M. R. New Windsor, Maryland.
Zimmerman, Gary. Manchester College, North Manchester, Indiana.

Introduction

The central theme of *Dwell in Peace: Applying Nonviolence to Everyday Relationships* is that human beings can be violated without their lives being taken by another. Killing another is certainly not the only way to violate a person's humanity. Violence is not something that happens only at gun point. It is present whenever the human dignity of an individual is oppressed, ignored, or abused. The purpose of this work is to reveal ways in which one can attempt to resolve interpersonal conflict without doing violence to another. In other words, the goal of this book is to announce ways of dealing with interpersonal conflict that are compatible with a nonviolent peacemaking life style.

Violence and conflict are daily occurrences, but these two happenings are not synonymous. A person can engage in conflict without violating another. The following three incidences reveal the presence of violence in everyday existence. The task of this book is to describe ways of recognizing such violence and dealing with it in a spirit of conflict rooted in nonviolent peacemaking.

Two former high school friends met at their twenty-fifth high school reunion for the first time since graduation. Joe talked about himself constantly, leaving no opportunity for Frank to talk. Yet, as these two men were about to leave, Joe said, "I'm glad all is well with you. Good luck. I'll see you at our next reunion." Joe felt his listener was all right, but he never gave Frank a chance to speak. Joe treated his listener as if he were an object. It did not really matter to Joe who he shared his life with, just as long as he could talk about himself. This type of behavior is a form of violence in that there is no recognition of the listener's personhood or uniqueness. Who the person is is not important; only that person's willingness to appear attentive is acknowledged. In this type of situation the human being is relegated to the status of a non-being, an object that is interchangeable with any other willing listener.

A husband and wife disagreed on where to vacation. This type of conflict is certainly legitimate and common. However, the husband had been taught that conflict is not healthy, so he gave in to his wife's desires without verbalizing his own preference. Throughout the trip the husband's ill feelings emerged in covert and subtle ways, through uncooperative and irritable behavior, rather than openly dealing with the conflict issue. In this example, the husband had violated not only his family, but himself. His uncooperative nature made it quite difficult for his family to enjoy themselves. Also, he had denied his own right to overtly state his opinion in a caring manner in an effort to achieve some agreeable resolution to the conflict.

A junior executive was in a meeting in which there was debate about the safety of a particular product the company was distributing. The president of the company overtly stated that he supported the sale of the product. However, one research chemist was concerned that not enough tests had been completed to be sure that the new product would be beneficial, rather than harmful to the public. The junior executive apparently was the only one who listened to this concern. She protested the sale and suggested delaying the marketing of this questionable product. This action contributed to the eventual loss of her job, while the product went on the market without adequate testing and was later recalled because of its harmful side effects. In this example, both the public and the junior executive were violated. The public was sold a harmful product and the junior executive lost her job, due to her decision not to support those in power when she felt they were unethical.

The aim of this work is to show that nonviolent peacemaking is applicable and helpful in understanding and dealing with conflicts, as in the above stated examples. What does it mean to treat another human being as an object? Is it possible to generate conflict by agreeing to another's wishes, when they are actually contrary to one's own desires? What does it mean to do what one feels is right when others are in total disagreement? Will one's lack of reward for such action destroy one's commitment? These are the types of concerns with which this book will deal.

The manner of discovering answers to questions such as the above, involved a dialogue between the author's understanding of human communication and interpersonal conflict and information gathered from forty-six representatives of the historic peace churches — Church of the Brethren, Quaker, and Mennonite. The statements offered in interviews by these forty-six individuals revealed important concerns and insights about interpersonal conflict. Some of their statements are used to illustrate particular ideas. The quotations are not individually footnoted in order for me to use them to exemplify points, without concern about misrepresenting a person's viewpoint. The themes and concepts that compose this book represent the author's understanding and viewpoint on interpersonal conflict from a peace tradition. The aim of this book is to provide some beginning guidelines for incorporating nonviolent peacemaking into one's interpersonal relationships and ways of handling conflict resolution.

Each chapter of this book points to ways in which interpersonal conflict can be understood and dealt with in a manner congruent with a nonviolent peacemaking orientation to human life. Part One, Living Within Peacemaking Limits, is centered around the notion that every human lives within limitations that he knowingly and/or unknowingly accepts. These limits may be called a variety of names, but each label points to the notion that humans manifest a particular style of living. As an individual accepts certain limitations, her life style will be different than a person who affirms other limits to her life. For example, to accept the solitary life of a hermit, a person limits his interaction with others. On the other hand, a person who accepts a gregarious style of living limits her time alone.

The contention that every life style has its own limitations can be tested by observing what happens when individuals go beyond the boundaries or limits of their present style of living. A career military person would probably go beyond the limitations of his life style if he failed to support his country in a time of war. A musician who refused to practice would soon discover a limit to her musical style of living. Thus, even though it is difficult to list all the limits of a particular life style, it is possible to describe some major themes. The goal of Part One is to announce some major themes that establish limits on the life styles of nonviolent peacemakers as they engage in interpersonal conflict.

Chapter One, Violence in Everyday Relationships, emphasizes that limitations in a nonviolent peacemaker's style of living are guided by the notion that violence occurs in all aspects of human life, including one's interpersonal life with others. For example, when one person ignores another, the other's humanity is not recognized; the dignity of the human requires recognition and affirmation. The nonviolent peacemaker's life style is limited by the desire not to violate another physically or psychologically. In interaction with another, one needs to at least recognize and affirm, not ignore, the other's humanity.

Chapter Two, The Modern Promethean or the Modern Job?, reveals another limitation in the peacemaker's life; he must seek compatibility of means and ends as he works for the goal of social justice. The modern Job, unlike the modern Promethean, cares for both oppressed and oppressor in order to maintain congruence of means and ends in the struggle for social justice. The nonviolent peacemaker is limited as she addresses an opponent in an interpersonal conflict situation. Nonviolent peacemaking does not legitimize tactics that care for the welfare of only one of the parties in the conflict situation.

Chapter Three, The Cost of Commitment, emphasizes that not all nonviolent peacemaking positions may be durable, because they have not been limited to a complete and realistic view of the human situation. Some individuals tend to ground their nonviolent peacemaking stance on the premise that love will always elicit a loving response from another. They do not understand the potential cost of a sincere and realistic peacemaking commitment. A lasting commitment to nonviolent peacemaking requires a person to recognize that a nonviolent and loving action may be met by a violent response. The nonviolent peacemaker must recognize that love does not always elicit a loving response as she attempts to resolve interpersonal conflict. Individuals must resist the temptation to base their nonviolent peacemaking orientation to interpersonal conflict on the premise that good actions will necessarily be rewarded by their fellows and/or opponents.

The second part of the book, Peacemaking Images in a Violent World, stresses that individuals are guided by only a partial understanding or incomplete view of the other. To grasp the totality of the person is an impossible achievement. The human being is a complex entity that is never fully knowable or understandable. Thus, images of the human are constructed in order to comprehend part of the mystery of the other. For example, in daily existence, common cliches such as, "He is a good fellow," or "I wouldn't turn my back on him," reveal that partial understandings of the person tend to direct one's understanding of others in everyday existence.

Both constructive and destructive views of the human are part of one's daily living. An individual may have an image of another that only recognizes the other's good characteristics. This might happen as an individual meets the person of his dreams. Initially in the relationship, the other can do no wrong. Only a recognition of goodness and compatibility guides one's understanding of the other. But as the two parties become better acquainted, an individual will likely notice flaws and inconsistencies in the other's behavior. The other may not have actually changed; rather, one's understanding of the other has become more realistic and inclusive of both constructive and negative characteristics. On the other hand, an individual may be informed that a particular person has a number of destructive attitudes and behaviors. A person may accept this information as accurate out of respect for a friend's opinion. Yet, if an individual has an open mind when meeting the "culprit," a much more positive image may develop. Thus, incomplete views of the human are part of daily existence in many ways; and a person's understanding of a particular person or group of people can change as new information guides and possibly redirects one's image of the other.

Chapter Four, The Roots of Violence, examines the contrasting traditional images of the human as inherently evil and innately good. Each of these viewpoints is critiqued and then combined in order to more fully reveal a realistic image of the human as having both constructive and destructive potentials. The nonviolent peacemaker needs to work to elicit good actions from others, but she must be prepared for the possibility of an opposite and even violent response.

An image or understanding of the person must include for the peacemaker the problem of conflict between humans. Chapter Five, The Inevitable Conflict, reveals that nonviolent peacemakers often have ambivalent reactions to conflict. However, an understanding of the person needs to incorporate a recognition of the inevitable nature of human conflict and the positive possibilities that may result from a conflict happening. In addition, one must recognize the risks to oneself and one's relationship to another whenever a conflict is confronted, even with the best of intentions. Conflict is necessary, inevitable, and also explosive at times.

Chapter Six, Caring—An Act of Power, announces the unavoidability of having and using power. Power is a necessary component in any image of the human being. Power is involved in acts of decision and action. As the familiar statement warns us: "To not decide is to decide." To decide to care or not to care is an act of power. To see power as a natural part of life allows the nonviolent peacemaker to choose modes of power that are compatible with peacemaking. Indeed, power used to coerce the other may be just another form of violence. But one cannot ignore the positive possibilities of power that, instead of seeking to do violence to the other, can be used to resist oppression. As nonviolent peacemakers develop an understanding of human relationships, they must recognize that power is not inherently evil and can be used in a manner congruent with the goal of nonviolent peacemaking.

Part Three, Peacemaking: A Radical Commitment, announces the potentially vulnerable stance of a peacemaker. One must commit oneself to what is believed to be right, even when such actions may limit one's own self-fulfillment. The radical commitment may at times require civil disobedience and a rejection of traditional societal rewards. Yet, as one works for what he perceives is right, an openness to opposing viewpoints must also be part of his peacemaking style. Commitment without openness is arrogance and eventual ignorance, because new sources of information have been ignored. On the other hand, the peacemaker must not be too easily persuaded. An affirmation of everyone's viewpoint is not a commitment at all; it is a naive escape from authentic responsibility. The goal for the peacemaker is to be committed, yet open to new views. She must attempt to confirm the other's personhood, but not necessarily embrace his ideas.

Chapter Seven, Commitment or Narcissism?, begins to ask questions about the nature of one's peacemaking commitment. Human beings knowingly and unknowingly commit themselves to activities and tasks for quite diverse reasons. Although usually no human is committed to any task for purely one reason alone, there are three general reasons for human commitment. First, a person may want to use a task or activity as a vehicle for her own fulfillment. Second, an individual may engage in an activity out of the belief that it is right and the hope that self-fulfillment may occur as a by-product of commitment. Third, a person may work for a particular goal because he feels it is right without concern for self-fulfillment. The preceding reasons for committing oneself to an activity or task are actually three ways of being-in-the-world. This chapter examines how each aids or hinders the goal of a just and peaceful world community. An individual can commit himself to nonviolent peacemaking for inappropriate reasons. The aim is to examine the reasons for one's commitment in the hope of gaining insight that can lead, if necessary, to a constructive behavior change.

Chapter Eight, From Independence to Interdependence, reveals that a peaceful world community may be given birth by a radical commitment that rejects the traditional contrasting options for relating with one another. Both collectivism and individualism need to be rejected as modes of relating with one another in interpersonal interaction. A genuine alternative to these traditional ways of associating must be sought. People must have concern for community, but community can only flourish where individual variances of opinion are respected and heard. Individuals need community to develop their interests; community requires individual challenges to avoid oppression and stagnation.

Chapter Nine, Confronting in Dialogue, announces that it is possible to confront another in a conflict situation in a manner that voices one's own opinion while affirming the other's personhood. Confrontation of another is not an uncommon happening. It occurs whenever a person feels wronged by another and makes her concern known to the other. For example, an individual may purchase a product from a salesman and later discover that it does not function adequately. The purchaser may then confront the seller and seek some form of reimbursement. A parent may confront her child for engaging in inappropriate behavior; or a child may confront his parent by describing an inconsistency in the parent's words and actions.

There are many methods of attempting to resolve a conflict after one has openly confronted the other. Some methods may attempt to destroy and/or humiliate the opponent. In war, the victor often demands an unconditional surrender from his enemy. In interpersonal relationships, the loser may be forced to apologize and then listen to questions such as, "Why did you do that to me?," "How could you have been so insensitive?," "Don't you care about anyone but yourself?" These types of statements leave little doubt in the minds of both parties as to who is the victor and the defeated. The following example reveals a method of conflict resolution that not only clearly defined the victor, but embarrassed and humiliated the loser.

A fourteen-year-old student was talking to a friend during a class period. In order to discipline the student, the teacher had the student apologize to the entire class. The teacher then had the student climb into a cardboard box and sit in full view of his peers. The other students in the class were encouraged to "discipline" this youth by throwing ping pong balls at him. When it was clear that the student truly regretted his actions, he was allowed to go back to his seat humiliated and embarrassed. The goal of this chapter is to reveal alternative methods of conflict resolution that do not seek to destroy or humiliate the opponent, and allow all parties in a dispute to be heard and respected.

The final chapter, The Dialogue of Peace, reveals the compatibility of Martin Buber's and Mahatma Gandhi's work. Although, these two men at times vehemently disagreed on conflict resolution methods, their combined efforts provide a set of conflict resolution guidelines that are necessary considerations for the nonviolent peacemaker. Both Buber and Gandhi worked to understand the opponent's viewpoint no matter how contrary it was to their own. This action may even change one's own opinion, or at least allow one to more fully understand the other's viewpoint.

In achieving a durable resolution the viewpoints of both parties need to be considered. An individual should not enter the conflict situation with a closed mind. As the nonviolent peacemaker works for a resolution, he must consider each party's perspective on an issue. The ultimate answer does not rest in any one person's understanding of the situation. A dialogical answer to a conflict emerges from "between" the opponents. This resolution is not a compromise or synthesis. It is not the possession of any one person. A dialogical resolution requires the combined efforts of two or more parties in dialogue.

This book is based on the knowledge that conflict is an inevitable and normal part of living that cannot and should not be eliminated. The task for the nonviolent peacemaker is to work to eliminate violence, not conflict, in interpersonal relationships. Learning to handle conflict and eliminate violence is necessary for the survival of humankind. Nonviolent peacemaking does not offer all the answers, but in conjunction with human dialogue perhaps a constructive alternative to violence is at least partially revealed.

Part One

Living Within Peacemaking Limits

Chapter One

Violence in Everyday Relationships

The nonviolent peacemaker affirms the sanctity of all human life. Taking the life of another is rejected as a means to solve conflict situations. One individual stated that he viewed human life as so sacred that he would lay down his life for others. Another person provided an example that clearly revealed concern for human life above and beyond one's own survival. As a pastor, he affirmed the importance of nonviolent peacemaking. Then one day he was beaten to unconsciousness and robbed. He was advised to to arm himself, but he refused. Nonviolent peacemaking was part of his life style that required him to respect the life of the other, even at his own expense. Yet another incident is of particular interest; it displays opposition to the military establishment due to the military's training to take human life in the solving of conflicts. The following transpired during a visit to a military basic training commencement:

> I had never been on a military base before. . . . We went into the auditorium, and I was . . . traumatized for a long time. . . . Well, the commencement speech was something else. All this was done in the name of God and call for Christ's blessings. But then every unit had to compete for the prize in cheerleading. [The winner was to develop the best] . . . kill cheer. And this went on—kill, kill, kill. And I was so distressed that when it came time for the national anthem, I simply could not rise out of my chair. . . . I was so sad.

Clearly, taking the life of another or training for such an action is not an acceptable means of resolving conflict within the framework of nonviolent peacemaking.

The Sanctity of Life

One representative of the historic peace churches, an historian, not only rejected physical violence as a means to resolve conflict, but expressed his personal opinion that those who embrace a just war theory are on historically shaky ground. No war has ever been justifiable; people just grow tired of seeking other options. He was then asked if war was necessary to stop the persecution of the Jewish people during World War II. His response was:

> Not to give Hitler an out, but if, for example, the United States had allowed full immigration there would never have been a massacre. . . . It is only deep into the war that extermination begins to occur. . . . In 1938-1939, it was very difficult for Jewish people to immigrate into this country. We had a depression in this country, and we didn't want those people coming in and taking our jobs. . . . We didn't want people who had no skills, but we did skim off a few professionals. . . . I don't meant to say that expelling people is the best solution . . . But I don't believe that carrying on a war is any less inhumane.

Kenneth Brown provides further insight into the peacemaker's view of the sanctity of life in the article "Updating Brethren Values: Rule Pacifism." He describes nonviolent peacemaking as a life stance that almost without question should reject the temptation to counter violence with more violence. Brown refers to nonviolent peacemaking as actively responding to evil and seeking reconciliation, instead of withdrawal. The response to conflict must be governed by a person's commitment to seek creative options for reconciliation that do not eliminate the other. However, for many people, the temptation is to operate from a utilitarian ethic and attempt to calculate the immediate effects of a nonviolent versus a violent response to evil. "They see that the immediate effects of suffering love do not overcome, as, indeed, often they do not. Christ could have drawn the same conclusion about his own work."[1] Brown contends that what the utilitarian ethic ignores or forgets is that a person cannot predict the future. The human is never sure if a nonviolent or violent action will be the most costly to humanity in the long run. Thus, Brown advocates the acceptance of rule pacifism.

> . . . rule pacifism is one facet of an ethical stance that does not take

into account consideration of the lesser of evils. . . . it brings to our consideration the longer, fuller view and therefore deems that breaking the rule against killing results in more extensive evil than keeping it, even though the immediate situation seems to result in the triumph of evil. Love may not win the day in a sinful world, but a different question must be posed: 'What fails the least. . . ?'[2]

The acceptance of nonviolent peacemaking as a rule limits a nonviolent peacemaker's repertoire of responses to violence and conflict. Elimination of a human is not an option. A short story by Ilse Aichinger, "The Bound Man," is analogous to the situation of the nonviolent peacemaker. In the story a man was robbed, knocked unconscious, and then securely bound. When the man awoke he discovered that he was no longer free, but bound by rope. He struggled valiantly against the rope, but to no avail. As time passed, the man regained some of his wit and patience. He found that he could actually move within the confines of the rope if he lifted each foot to the right height and distance then placed his foot on the ground before the rope tightened. Eventually, the bound man found that movement within the confines of the rope allowed him more freedom than he had even thought possible in such a situation.

[He found that if] . . . he remained entirely within the limits set by his rope he was free of it, it did not confine him, but gave him wings and endowed his leaps and jumps with purpose; just as the flights of birds of passage have purpose when they take wing in the warmth of summer and hesitantly make small circles in the sky.[3]

The nonviolent peacemaker is bound like the man in Ilse Aichinger's short story. The story reveals a man constrained by physical material. The nonviolent peacemaker is also constrained, but by the commitment not to take the life of another in the resolving of conflict. Like the bound man, the nonviolent peacemaker seeks to find freedom within limits. The nonviolent peacemaker's quest is to discover creative approaches to conflict situations that are compatible with the self-imposed limits of nonviolent peacemaking.

Gene Sharp, in *Politics of Nonviolent Action,* reveals that it is possible to creatively pursue approaches to conflict happenings within nonviolent peacemaking limits. In Norway in 1942, during Nazi occupation, Vidkun Quisling, the Norwegian fascist Minister-President, attempted to establish a Corporate State that emulated Mussolini's Italy. To gain control of the educational facilities, Quisling required compulsory membership in a new teacher's organization. The head of *Hird,* the Norwegian storm troopers, was appointed the leader of the mandatory membership group that advocated fascist ideals. Of the country's twelve thousand teachers, more than eighty percent signed their names and addresses to a petition that stated their refusal to teach fascist values. This correspondence was forwarded to the Education Department under Quisling's command, and the government retaliated by closing the schools. The teachers were not deterred; they held classes in their private homes. Quisling then had one thousand male teachers arrested, tortured, and held in concentration camps. The schools reopened and the remaining teachers overtly repudiated their membership in the fascist organization. Because of this tactic, the arrested teachers were shipped " . . . on cattle trains and overcrowded steamers . . . to a camp near Kirkenes, in the Far North. . . . The teachers were kept at Kirkenes in miserable conditions, doing dangerous work."[4] This action inspired the teachers at home to increase their resistance.

The culmination of the teachers' protest occurred one day at a school near Oslo where Quisling raged, " . . . You teachers have destroyed everything for me!"[5] In less than eight months, the arrested teachers returned home as heros and Quisling's dream of a Corporate State was ordered abandoned by Hitler. There is no guarantee that nonviolent peacemaking will always be effective. But the struggle of the Norwegian teachers points to the importance of affirming the sanctity of life by attempting to answer the question of violence with creative responses within the confines of nonviolent peacemaking.

Recognizing and Limiting Interpersonal Violence

Nonviolent peacemaking is not applicable to international conflict situations alone. Nonviolent peacemaking establishes boundaries for virtually every level of conflict with others. Allen Deeter, Director of Peace Studies at Manchester College, stated that nonviolent peacemaking is a commitment to a reconciling and peacemaking way of life. This involves every level of existence, from interpersonal relationships, to institutions, and international conflicts. Another individual said, "My personal definition of pacifism requires one to settle all difficulties in a peaceful way, regardless of whether those difficulties be in war between nations, between individuals, between members of the family, in institutions, or churches . . . "

Nearly all of the representatives of the historic peace churches referred to nonviolent peacemaking as inclusive of more than just opposition to the use of military force to solve problems on an international level. They contended that if a nonviolent peacemaker rejects the use of violence on a physical level, he must then develop a life style that makes the use of violence unnecessary. This recognition of violence in everyday living is summarized by one person who remembered a strong opposition to war and to the use of violence in interpersonal relationships in his peace church during his youth:

> To me pacifism is a philosophy of life with a strong emphasis on agape love, reconciliation, and forgiveness, in opposition to force and violence in interpersonal as well as international relationships. . . . I remember periodically the church would be called into counsel on such questions as should a member of the church have the privilege of going to law in certain legal procedures. . . . And also, the very strong emphasis of the deacon visit, when the deacons would come into the home and ask you, 'Are you, as far as you know, at peace and harmony with your brethren and sisters in the church?' And I especially remember my father's answer would always be, 'As far as I know, and if anybody knows otherwise, I would certainly welcome this information.' Because he was deeply concerned that he would be living in this proper relationship with his fellow man.

Violence permeates all levels of human life. Yet most nonviolent peacemaking literature has been limited to describing alternative responses to physical violence. Little has been revealed about covert personal violence when an individual attempts to manipulate the other and harm him psychologically. The representatives of the historic peace churches provided some initial guidelines for understanding this problem. One person stated that he attempted to minimize the psychological violence done to another. Another individual said he attempted to avoid doing irreversible harm to another psychologically.

Anything that limits the psychological or physical growth of another in a destructive manner is an act of personal violence. Non-violent peacemaking values the other and attempts to encourage each person's human growth. The peacemaker needs to build up the other and to seek a creative end to conflict that does not tear down people or cultures. One individual summarized this viewpoint by stating that: " . . . pacifism is a concept where the dignity of all mankind is never reduced in any shape, way or faction. [My pacifism impels me not] . . . to try to reduce the dignity of another person."

To ensure another's psychological growth and human dignity, proper human attention must be given. Examples of feral children, raised among animals, who have not acquired the social characteristics of humanness, demonstrate the importance of human contact. The need for human attention is also revealed through a disease known as "hospitalism" which affects small infants. The babies tend to atrophy and die if human attention is not granted them.

For a human to grow and mature, contact with others is essential.

Watzlawick, Beavin and Jackson provide a theoretical under-standing of what happens to a human being when attention is given and when it is denied. According to their analysis, an individual can respond to another in one of three ways. First, a person can confirm the other. The human communicates with others for more than an ex-change of information. He also relates with others to become aware of his own individual being. In fact, this is the premise that many counseling theories are built upon; the client comes to know herself as the counselor accepts or confirms the client as she is. Second, an in-dividual can reject another. This means that an individual recognizes the presence of the other, but does not care to pursue even a limited relationship. The person is acknowledged, but he is not invited or ac-cepted into a human encounter. Third, a person can disconfirm another, which happens when he responds to another as if she did not exist. William James is quoted as saying: "No more fiendish punish-ment could be divised, even were such a thing physically possible, than that one should be turned loose in society and remain absolutely un-noticed by all the members thereof."[6] Disconfirmation robs the in-dividual of needed social interaction. The individual becomes alienated from her own self because she is constantly ignored as if she did not even exist.

Disconfirmation is a potent form of covert personal violence that happens in everyday living. This game is often played in high school. A group of fellows who have a close relationship may intentionally walk by another individual, who is not part of their clique, without even acknowledging his existence. Some persons in our culture have witnessed the power of disconfirmation and use it as a technique to promote behavior change. A college professor was asked a variety of questions regarding her grading system. Comments that questioned the legitimacy of her grading procedure were ignored, as if they had never been raised.

The cry during the 1960s by many Black protestors was, "I am Somebody." Black men and women rebelled against the covert per-sonal violation of disconfirmation. Martin Luther King, Jr. stated his hope for Black Americans in "Let Us Be Dissatisfied." "This is our hope for the future, and with this faith we will be able to sing in some not too distant tomorrow with a cosmic past tense, 'We have over-come, we have overcome, deep in my heart, I did believe we would overcome.' "[7] Social, economic, and political prejudice needed to be erased for King's dream to materialize. But his campaign for human rights also promoted movement toward another fundamental change. Black men and women no longer accepted disconfirmation. Martin

Luther King, Jr. had allowed black people to announce their humanity.

> Ten years ago, Negroes seemed almost invisible to the larger society, and the facts of their harsh lives were unknown to the majority of the nation. . . . In this decade of change, the Negro stood up and confronted his oppressor. He faced the bullies and the guns, the dogs and the tear gas. He put himself squarely before the vicious mobs and moved with strength and dignity toward them and decisively defeated them. . . . We gained manhood in the nation that had always called us "boy". . . . For this, we can feel a legitimate pride. [8]

Martin Luther King, Jr. led the way for black people to reclaim their humanity and reject the ignoring glance of disconfirmation. One of the fundamental lessons of the 1960s was that violence interpersonally results when a human is present and not seen, when she speaks and is not heard, and when he looks for a human bond with another, only to meet the ignoring depths of disconfirmation. Personal violence can be limited by acknowledging the other's humanity, which disconfirmation ignores.

Affirming Human Worth and Significance

Viewing people as objects is another means of relating that often violates their humanity. When individuals are treated as objects their humanity is forgotten. The human situation today can be defined by stating that technical sophistication has generated an atmosphere that has increased the tendency to view the human as an object. Technique, rather then human concern, seems to typify the present century. James W. Douglass in *The Non-Violent Cross: A Theology of Revolution and Peace* has stated that civilization has become typified by the machine, rather than the human. Technical calculation has become a pseudonym for truth in the twentieth century. If the technical knowledge is available, a new invention is produced and invented with little concern about whether it should be developed. "We have become, in the words of Jacques Ellul, the foremost analyst of this phenomenon, a 'civilization of means'. . . . As men of technique we are actually incapable of seeking truth in any other context . . ."[9] Perhaps Orwell's *Nineteen Eighty-four* and Huxley's *Brave New World* do indeed prophesy the results of a technique-oriented society. It seems that many people have lost sight of their human values and have invested their energy in a one-sided emphasis on technique. Often the major question "Should a particular chemical or weapon be invented?" is not asked. The twentieth century tends to operate under the assumption that something should be created or accomplished because it is technically feasible. If it is possible to develop nuclear weapons, they must be developed even if they might annihilate human life. Technical sophistication allows the human to ignore questions regarding the rightness of actions. As war and killing become more technologically sophisticated, the individual is increasingly displaced from the results of his actions. Pushing a button to drop a bomb or release a nuclear device loses the personal horror of hand-to-hand combat.

An individual can also distance himself from the enemy by treating him as a nonhuman entity, an object. Robert Jay Lifton, in "The 'Gook Syndrome' and 'Numbed Warfare,'" refers to objectification of the enemy as a psychological technique used to ignore the humanity of the other. Individuals are reduced to nonhuman status— Japs, Krauts, Commies, or Gooks—a person sees no likeness to himself in those he attempts to eliminate. Lifton believes that American men who fought in the Vietnam War participated in a "Gook Syndrome." The American soldiers did not kill North Vietnamese or NFL guerrillas; rather they worked to annihilate the Gooks. Where the term Gook originated linguistically is difficult to determine, but the result of using such labels is quite apparent. Individual differences tend to be ignored; the enemy is objectified to a nonhuman status.[10]

Objectification of the other is not an isolated condition due only to war; it is a common occurence in daily living. For example, a nonviolent peacemaker could objectify all who disagree with her view of the world as hawkish violators of human dignity; or the proponents of violence, in the effort to counter lawlessness and wrong, may objectify all nonviolent peacemakers into a category of unpatriotic cowards.

Objectification of a person occurs frequently in human relationships. For instance, a woman who is attempting to promote attitudinal change toward the roles of women in society may be objectified into the category of a radical feminist. To objectify the woman is to cease to respond to another human being; objectifiers only respond to their prejudices regarding an abstract objectified category, feminist. The actual human person is not encountered. But the woman who desires to promote change regarding women's roles can also objectify all those who disagree with her as male chauvinists or ignorant housewives. Thus, both the person who seeks change and those who support the status quo can ignore others by objectifying them into a category that denies their humanity.

When those who seek change objectify supporters of the status quo, an either/or form of thought emerges—"Either you are with us, or you oppose us." This same mode of thinking occurs when those in power objectify all those who question their decisions by categorizing them as subversive influences. Robert D. Nye, in his work entitled *Conflict Among Humans*, refers to this dichotomous form of thought as a "neanderthal mentality." He claims that these individuals are highly ethnocentric; they judge others by their own standards without attempting to understand the other's viewpoint. This form of logic denies the complexity of issues and leads to undifferentiated judgments and the categorization of people.[11] The either/or thinking was used by Hitler to a tactical advantage. Hitler was able to build an image of the heroic as Aryan and an image of non-Aryan or Jewish-dominated as immoral and destructive. Everything was then judged as either good, Aryan, or destructive, non-Aryan. Either/or thinking deals with the other as an objectified image, Gook, non-Aryan, or feminist — the common humanity of the other is ignored.

Individuals can limit personal violence that others direct at them by not allowing others' objectified images of them control their actions. A person can become more concerned about the other's image of him than the rightness of an action or movement. It seems that the hallmark of our society is often to conform, not to seek creative new ideas and approaches to human life. Indeed, it is tempting to engage in actions because they are marketable or saleable and to ignore the question of whether what one is doing is right. However, a nonviolent peacemaker must sometimes engage in the behavior she believes is right, regardless of the perceptions of the rest of society. For example, interviewee Desmond Bittinger stated the importance of redefining manliness and womanliness as standing one's own ground and speaking with clarity and compassion without dominating another. A nonviolent peacemaker may need to voice support for issues and causes that are not necessarily marketable or conforming to the ongoing social structure. To be controlled by an objectified image of oneself is to limit one's ability to take stands that are unpopular, but nevertheless necessary.

To affirm the sanctity of life in daily interpersonal interactions, the human needs to limit the personal violence done to others and himself. This requires an individual to recognize the humanity of the other, rather than respond to an objectified image. Also, one may need to reject the other's objectified image of oneself in order to voice a nonviolent alternative in a violent world. One representative of the historic peace churches clearly endorsed this idea.

> I conceptualize pacifism as involving a life style in which one's daily interactions with others . . . are affected. I think physical violence tends to come about when violence of other kinds have preceded it. That is, I define violence as treating people like things and one can have various states of treating people like things which culminate in physical violence. . . . you already have failed when things get to the physical level. You should have started a lot sooner, in working out harmonious life styles.

Physical violence is but one realm of violence. Covert personal violence happens when disconfirmation and objectification of the human occur. Failure to acknowledge the other may violate his human dignity. And to respond to an objectified image of the other or to allow the other's unchanging image of oneself to limit one's own actions violates the humanness of both parties in a conflict.

Chapter Two

The Modern Promethean
or the Modern Job?

The effectiveness and success of a peacemaking stance cannot always be assured; therefore, something more fundamental must inspire one to accept a nonviolent peacemaking position. One representative of the historic peace churches said his primary consideration was the sacredness of human life. He was not as concerned with the effectiveness of nonviolent peacemaking as he was with its rightness or truthfulness. Another person stated that he affirmed a nonviolent peacemaking life style because it was right, not because he was certain it would succeed. Dale Brown stated in an interview that at one time he was a humanistic or political pacifist who felt that pacifism could succeed in almost any situation. He now considers that position naive and is committed to the pacifist position because he feels it is right, not because it will always be effective. Nonviolent peacemaking embraces the concept of the cross and accepts the fact it may not be effective at all times.

> . . . a word from Art Gish is appropriate . . . we are called to live correctly . . . and not called to succeed. . . . I don't guarantee for example, that if everyone were a pacifist that the United States would continue to exist as it is.

An individual needs a firmer ground than effectiveness if her nonviolent peacemaking stance is to endure. This does not minimize the potential effectiveness of nonviolent peacemaking, which has been documented by Gene Sharp in *The Politics of Nonviolent Action: Part One Power and Struggle;* rather, effectiveness is a secondary consideration to the rightness or truthfulness of a behavior or action.

Truth as Touchstone

For many nonviolent peacemakers truthfulness, not effectiveness, is the primary criterion in nonviolent peacemaking. Truth is embraced as the value that undergirds nonviolent peacemaking. However, truth as a basis for nonviolent peacemaking must not be relativistic or absolutistic. One individual stated that he believed that human values were much more than pure relativism; pure relativism would mean that the words right and wrong are virtually meaningless. Yet another person emphasized his concern that rigid or absolutistic values can legitimize an individual's behavior too much, even to the extent of waging war. The possibility of a value orientation that is neither relativistic nor absolutistic is pointed to even more directly by the following comments:

> . . . relativists are never really relativists. They are encompassed by all kinds of values. . . . [Yet] I'm probably scared of orthodoxy and dogma as much as anyone, but on the other hand, I think the social context in which human beings live is just so loaded with values that there is no way one can really escape it.

Neither a relativistic understanding of values nor a dogmatic orientation is an appropriate way of understanding the notion of truth for the nonviolent peacemaker.

Mahatma Gandhi based his work and life on the principle of truth. In his South African campaigns Gandhi used the phrase "passive resistance" to describe his nonviolent peacemaking activities. But he was not satisfied with that terminology.

> [One individual suggested that Gandhi call his approach to nonviolent peacemaking] . . . 'sadagraha', meaning 'firmness in a good cause'. [Gandhi's response was] I liked the word, but it did not fully represent the whole idea I wished to connote. I therefore corrected it to 'Satyagraha'. Truth (Satya) implies love and firmness (Agraha) engenders and therefore serves as a synonym for force. I thus began to call the Indian movement 'Satyagraha', that is to say the Force which is born of Truth and Love or non-violence, and gave up the use of the phrase 'passive resistance' . . .[1]

Throughout Gandhi's campaigns, he seemed to have a clear

vision of Truth. But his understanding of Truth was not dogmatic or absolutistic or even consensually verifiable at times. An absolutistic understanding of truth often locates truth in a dogma or ideology. It is a pre-established truth that allows little openness to new truth or revelation. Consensually verifiable truth allows public opinion or repeatable experimentation to determine the truth of an idea or happening. The larger the quantity of collaborators on a particular truth, the more certain one can be of its truth. However, truth is not always absolute or consensually verifiable; quite often it emerges in the uniqueness of the situation. As a truth emerges it may or may not be recognized by large numbers of people.

Erik Erikson believed that Mahatma Gandhi had an emergent conception of truth, which required him to immerse himself in dialogue with the situation, in order to apprehend the truth that emerged "between" him and the situation. Erikson further says:

> . . . there is no reason to question the fact that the sudden conviction that the moment of truth *had* arrived always came upon him as if from a voice which had spoken before he had quite listened. Gandhi often spoke of his inner voice, which would speak unexpectedly in the preparedness of silence — but then with irreversible firmness and an irresistible demand for commitment. . . . That is, the moment of truth is suddenly there — unannounced and pervasive in its stillness. But it comes only to him who has lived with facts and figures in such a way that he is always ready for sudden synthesis and will not, from sheer surprise and fear, startle truth away.[2]

Gandhi's truth could not be located in a dogma isolated from the situation; Gandhi encountered the concrete living happening to discover the truth that emerged between himself and the situation. Erikson believed that Gandhi only committed himself to a relative truth,[3] but Erikson's understanding of Gandhi's truth is somewhat misleading. A relativistic truth is subjective, in that each person makes an internal judgment of what is truth and falsity; but no judgment can be made to call one view of truth more appropriate than another. Each person's internal or subjective view of the world is accepted; thus, Truth becomes relative in that no one understanding of an event is more right or wrong than anyone else's view of an event. Surely Gandhi did not totally believe that his cause was no more truthful than the oppressor's. He affirmed his understanding of Truth enough to suffer and die for it. Thus, both an absolutistic or dogmatic and a relativistic understanding of Gandhi's truth is inadequate.

Joan Bondurant, in her analysis of Gandhi, relates that Gandhi's understanding of truth was neither absolutistic nor totally relative.

Bondurant states:

> . . . the problem of objectivity is solved in the Gandhian method. While admitting truth to be relative, some objective measure is established. The solution is in terms of 'man, the measure. . . . ' Individual man searches for truth in terms of the community of which he is a part. 'The quest for Truth,' said Gandhi cannot be 'prosecuted in a cave.'[4]

Gandhi did not accept an absolutistic or objective view of truth. However, he did establish some criteria. His emergent truth incorporated the views of the human community, which included both oppressed and oppressor. As Bondurant notes, this is neither an absolutistic nor purely relative view of truth.

Maurice Friedman, in *Touchstones of Reality: Existential Trust and the Community of Peace,* refers to a touchstone of reality as an alternative view of truth that rejects absolutism and subjectivism or relativism. Friedman's concept of truth gives a label to Gandhi's truth that does not seem to fit in traditional categories of absolutistic or relativistic. Friedman uses the term touchstone as a metaphor to refer to the ground on which one stands from which one presently views the world or apprehends a truth. Touchstone means that an individual will probably not remain forever on the same ground that affirms a truth; a person is open to new understandings of truth. Clearly, Friedman is pointing to something other than an absolutistic view of truth. Thus, the metaphor is appropriate to Gandhi in that he rejected a dogmatic view of truth, as Erikson and Bondurant have described.

The metaphor also rejects a relativistic or subjectivistic view of truth. This is again congruent with what Bondurant pointed to, as she stressed that Gandhi's truth was not totally relative. A touchstone of reality is not a relative truth that is dependent on one's subjective view or personal projection; it is the result of dialogue when the human comes into contact with the situation. The truth emerges from "between" the person and the situation. Truth is not present *in* an abstract dogma, *in* the person, or *in* the situation; rather, truth emerges from the "between" of what an individual touches or encounters. The truth that emerges from the between of a situation is the human's touchstone of reality or ground on which he stands or interprets the world. Friedman is pointing to a concrete understanding of truth that does not leave one groping in a sea of relativism or mindlessly clinging to an abstract dogma.[5] Friedman's touchstone of reality provides a label for Gandhi's emergent understanding of truth. Gandhi's truth is revealed between the oppressor and oppressed. Gandhi's touchstone of reality is a truth that does not give a person the luxury of interpreting a situation from a pre-established dogmatic truth, nor does it give a person the option of believing that truth is subjectively unique to each person and therefore only relative. A touchstone is a truth that emerges between oneself and the situation, or in Gandhi's case, between oppressor and oppressed.

Both Friedman and Gandhi recognized that every emergent touchstone or truth is based on a limited looking at the ongoing happening. Truth as touchstone may even be the incorrect avenue to a full understanding of truth. This leaves a person with the task of committing herself to a limited understanding of truth; yet only by committing herself to her touchstone can an individual discover the rightness or error in her own emergent view of truth. Gandhi emphasized the necessity of commitment to an individual's touchstone of reality in order to test it for its truthfulness.

> But how is one to realize this Truth. . . . By single-minded devotion (abbyasa) and indifference to every other interest in life (vairagya)—replies the Bhagavad Gita. In spite, however, of such devotion, what may appear as truth to one person will often appear as untruth to another person. But this need not worry the seeker. . . . there is nothing wrong in everyone following Truth according to one's lights. Indeed it is one's duty to do so. Then if there is a mistake on the part of any one so following Truth, it will automatically be set right. . . . [if] one takes to the wrong path one stumbles, and is this redirected to the right path.[6]

Gandhi calls for commitment to an individual's touchstone of reality or current understanding of truth that has emerged between himself and the situation. He also emphasizes that a person's touchstone may lead him astray from truth. Thus, an individual is left to live a double action of commitment and openness to new revelations or touchstones of reality.

Means—The End in the Making

As a number of representatives of the historic peace churches related their observations about the ongoing happenings of the world, a truth or touchstone emerged, the need for social justice. One individual said that the human must learn to limit self-interest by giving up the concept of nationality and moving toward an international understanding of world justice. Another person stated that there will be immense violence unless we overcome the disparity between rich and poor. He visualized the riots during the 1960s as only minor incidents compared to what may erupt in the 1980s unless we work on the question of social justice in a direct and deliberate fashion. One individual stated that his understanding of nonviolent peacemaking reached across all liberation movements. Nonviolent peacemaking incorporates a cry for human justice. The dilemma comes when an individual apprehends a concrete emergent truth or touchstone, the need for social justice, and must decide how to implement or deal with it within the framework of nonviolent peacemaking. Paul Keller stated the problem quite succinctly:

> ... I'm faced with the question: Does my concern for ... justice require that I engage in violent solutions?. ... My own answer to that is that I do not think that inferior means can produce superior ends. ... to engage in a violent response to violent treatment is to compound the problem rather than solve it.

For the peacemaker, in the implementation of a truth both the ends and means must be compatible. There is little choice but to seek nonviolent means, if the means are to be congruent with the end goal of a peaceful world.

The compatibility of means and ends is not a new revelation, yet it still provides helpful guidance when a nonviolent peacemaker attempts to put a truth into action. Mahatma Gandhi emphasized the necessary compatibility of means and ends; this principle is one of the fundamental bases of Satyagraha. Concern for using the appropriate means to achieve a truthful end is clearly stated by Gandhi himself:

> They say "means are after all means." I would say "means are after all everything." As the means so the end. There is no wall of separation between means and end. Indeed the Creator has given us control (and that too very limited) over means, none over the end. Realization of the goal is in exact proportion to that of the means. This is a proposition that admits of no exception.[7]

Martin Luther King, Jr. was impressed by Gandhi's Satyagraha, which used nonviolence as the means for implementing truth. Nonviolence puts into practice a means of protest that voices the rights of the oppressed and yet does not destroy the rights of the oppressor. Gandhi and King had a concern for human life that embraced both the oppressed and oppressor. This view of human existence is expressed quite clearly by Albert Schweitzer's well known notion of "reverence for life." Nonviolent peacemaking is a means that is compatible with the ends of truth, reverence for life; it respects both the life of the oppressed and the oppressor. Thomas Merton, when commenting on the importance of Gandhi's Satyagraha, said that liberation of both oppressed and oppressor is the goal of Gandhi's means to truth. A violent change is not a change at all; only the actors have changed parts.[8]

The compatibility of means and ends is not accepted by everyone. A number of former political pacifists who once thought pacifism could change the world have since embraced more pragmatic stances. "The Pilgrimage of an Ex-Pacifist" by Gordon Shull states quite openly that he rejected pacifism because it does not deal with the pragmatic realities of the ongoing world.[9] Dale Brown points to similar defections of Brethren pacifists to the ranks of nonpacifism in his work entitled *Brethren and Pacifism*.[10] These rejections of nonviolent peacemaking do not necessarily mean that a former nonviolent peacemaker has altered the goal of achieving a peaceful world. He may have assumed a different means of achieving the previously recognized goal. This points to a fundamental disagreement between those who see violence as a means and those who conceptualize nonviolence as a means to the same goal, a peaceful world.

Approaches to Change: Peacemaking or Violence?

A distinction between violent and nonviolent means to the goal of a peaceful world can be conceptualized by understanding the problem of change. The book, *Change: Principles of Problem Formation and Problem Resolution* by Watzlawick, Weakland, and Fisch, provides a theoretical system from which two types of change, or means of getting to an end, can be viewed: (1) First-order change or means involves a change within a pre-established system. It is change that does not usually make a significant difference; there is a change of roles, but no change in the system occurs. (2) Second-order change is a recalibration of the system. It is change outside the system and does produce a significant difference.[11] For example, if people are oppressed by others and a rebellion occurs only to change the roles of oppressed and oppressor, then first-order change has transpired. But if an individual rejects the oppressed label and protests nonviolently while still caring for the oppressor, a second-order change is given life; the one-up and one-down understanding of the world is rejected. The desire is no longer to switch roles, but to creatively carve out new roles that can be mutually beneficial to both oppressed and oppressor. The old system is rejected; a second-order change is promoted. In order to implement the perceived truth of social justice in a manner that is compatible with nonviolent peacemaking, a person needs to seek second-order rather than first-order change. First-order change merely reverses the roles of the actors in the current system of oppressor and oppressed. Second-order change works to constitute a new system that may liberate both parties in the conflict.

Further clarification of the difference between change *within* the system (first-order change) and change *of* the system itself (second-order change) is pointed to by Rollo May. In his book, *Power and Innocence: A Search for the Sources of Violence,* May refers to the film, *The Wild Child,* which was a re-enactment of an actual happening in the eighteenth century. A doctor attempted to teach a boy who had lived a number of years in a forest as an animal to be human. The boy learned to speak in an elementary, chopped fashion, but otherwise he made little progress. In a dire moment of discouragement, the doctor decided that there was one test that should reveal if the boy was human—" . . . will the boy fight back when he is unjustly punished?"[12] Knowing that the boy accepted punishment, being enclosed in a closet when he had misbehaved, the doctor shut the boy in the closet when he had correctly completed an assignment. In a burst of righteous indignation, the boy put up a valiant struggle. And with a feeling of great relief, the doctor recognized a central element of humanness in the boy. The capacity to stand against injustice is a distinguishing characteristic of the human person. According to Rollo May, the human is born to rebel against the inhuman and unjust.

A number of the representatives of the historic peace churches were concerned about the need to promote social justice. Their statements corresponded with May's statement that it is natural for humans to struggle against injustice. They not only saw a need to rebel against injustice done against themselves, but they announced a desire to right injustice done to others as well. Howard Richards stated his concern about human injustice:

> . . . identification with the poor makes me a pacifist, because I think the poor tend to be the powerless, and the powerless tend to benefit from a system where power is subordinated to moral considerations. . . . I think that peace and justice are so closely interrelated that one can almost say that they're two words for the same thing. And I've come to think that peaceful means are the most likely ways to achieve peace as well as being desirable in themselves.

Rollo May contends that there are two responses to injustice, the revolutionary and the rebel, which correspond to the distinction between first-order and second-order change, respectively. He states that the revolutionary wants to enact an external change of the governing structure. Often a revolution substitutes one form of government for another, leaving the individual citizen no better off than before. The rebel does not want to exchange roles with the oppressor—her concern is to change the system itself.

> The slave who kills his master is an example of the revolution-
> ary. He can then only take his master's place and be killed in turn by
> later revolutionaries. But the rebel is the one who realizes that the
> master is as much imprisoned, if not as painfully, as he is by the in-
> stitution of slavery; he rebels against the system which permits
> slaves and masters. His rebellion, if successful, saves the master also
> from the indignity of owning slaves.[13]

The revolutionary is encapsulated within the very system he protests
against. When he usurps power from the oppressor, a first-order
change is promoted. The rebel wants to promote a change in the
system itself; she strives for a second-order change that will eliminate
the relationship of oppressed and oppressor.

The revolutionary is only concerned with outer restraints imposed
upon him by those in power. The rebel operates with built-in restraints
that are self-imposed. The rebel has a vision of the ideal world or life,
which allows her to transcend petty pride, revenge, and win/lose situations. The rebel has compassion for all people, including the oppressor. Openness in dialogue, which allows the other to be heard and
herself sometimes to be swayed, typifies the rebel. The rebel attempts
to invite a new world, not one of oppressed and oppressor, but of concern for each. A nonviolent peacemaker in the rebel role accepts the
humanity and right to live of both oppressor and oppressed. Concern
for both parties restrains her enthusiasm while attempting to implement her own perception of truth or touchstone. The process followed
in the promotion of truth will require the revolutionary to become
another oppressor and will allow the rebel to attempt to creatively
carve out new roles of cooperation and co-existence. A violent revolution is a first-order change—only the roles are exchanged. A nonviolent peacemaking rebellious role works to change the system that
requires an oppressor/oppressed relationship. The goal is to avoid a
change that, in the words of one individual, merely " . . . decides who
is to be master and who the subject or slave."

Maurice Friedman provides additional material that can be related to the means-oriented approach of nonviolent peacemaking and
the ends-conscious tactics of violent confrontation. Friedman does
not use the terms rebel and revolutionary in the same manner as May,
but he points to a similar difference in approaches to achieving
change. Friedman differentiates between the Modern Job and the
Modern Promethean. The Modern Job both confronts or rebels while
still confirming his opponent. The Modern Job works to change the

system of human relationships that posits one human over another. The Modern Promethean sees no such option as possible; he feels he must rebel to gain the reigns of power or submit to mastery. Friedman conceives the Modern Job as concerned with changing the entire system, not just becoming a ruler himself; he attempts to affirm the other even in the act of rebellion.

Often when an individual reads the biblical account of Job he does not see rebellion, but mere conformity to God's will. This interpretation does great injustice to what actually transpired between Job and God. In Chapter 9, Job indicts God with almost unparallelled bitterness; Job is rebelling, not withdrawing. But his rebellion is one based in dialogue. Job boldly states:

> 'He may slay me, I await it' . . . 'But I will argue my ways before him.' The key to Job and what makes him the prototype of . . . the Modern Job is the fact that he trusts *and* contends, that the two go together, that his contending with God takes place in dialogue with God, and in that dialogue he stands his ground.[14]

This double action of trust and contending makes the Modern Job the strongest rebel possible; he holds his ground and confirms the other, in order to bring about a fundamental second-order change rather than implement a new tyranny.

Maurice Friedman considers Martin Luther King, Jr. to be the embodiment of a Modern Job. In dialogue he worked for change, but still cared for the oppressor. When King's house was bombed, he implored his followers to practice love and nonviolence, not revenge. When J. Edgar Hoover referred to him as a liar, King's response was to remark about the difficulty of Hoover's work, rather than refute the statements or question the FBI Director's character. In the fall of 1966, King saw that he could not separate civil rights from opposition to the Vietnam War; thus he began to speak out against the war — against the advice of his counselors. He was ready to sacrifice his influence and prestige, rather than follow the route of expediency.[15] Martin Luther King, Jr., the Modern Job, was concerned with responding to the touchstone or truth that emerged between him and the situation, adhering to compatibility of means and ends, and caring for both the oppressor and oppressed. In short, his style of nonviolent peacemaking points to the importance of achieving a truthful end through adherence to means that care for both oppressor and oppressed.

Chapter Three

The Cost of Commitment

Representatives of the historic peace churches collectively announced that nonviolent peacemaking does not always ensure victory in a violent world, and is often viewed by others as a foolish and naive stance toward violence. Indeed, some individuals believed that nonviolent peacemaking may result in so little reward that it is difficult for some to maintain their nonviolent peacemaking position. One person offered an insight into why some nonviolent peacemaking groups did not endure after the 1960s and early 1970s.

> I don't believe that a pacifism based on pragmatic grounds will be durable. The 60s was a strange phenomenon for me. Before this, I had visualized pacifism as a tiny minority view. This view has been quite ephemeral in two respects: (1) many people changed to traditional views after the war, and (2) many people easily accepted the idea of violent revolution for the oppressed when they saw that nonviolence was not immediately effective. An enduring pacifism needs a commitment that transcends pragmatism. . . . One can't demonstrate that pacifism can exist pragmatically. One can't experiment with pacifism without being committed to it, because the ultimate commitment requires the giving of one's life.

Another person said that he did not believe that all forms of nonviolent peacemaking could endure hardship and nonresults. The optimistic view that love always elicits a loving response from the other is not as lasting as a biblical understanding of nonviolent peacemaking, which does not base its commitment solely on results. At times, it may be necessary to offer love to another without any expectation of being appreciated for one's efforts.

Nonviolent peacemakers are often the recipients of wrath from "pragmatic realists," such as Reinhold Niebuhr, who contended that the depth of human evil sometimes must be met with a violent response. At one point in his life, Niebuhr supported the nonviolent peacemaking position, but he later rejected it as too idealistic to deal with crises such as Mussolini's Italy and Hitler's Germany. Niebuhr became a vocal critic of the optimistic view of the human being, which contended that love would always be rewarded over evil. He did not accept the premise that even the most vile person could be changed, if one had enough time, patience, and love. Reinhold Niebuhr saw this approach as naive and ignorant of the depth of human evil. The promoter of love may not only be rebuked, but actually lose his life.[1]

Indeed, Niebuhr's argument cannot be overlooked. Such persons as Jesus Christ, Mahatma Gandhi, and Martin Luther King, Jr. advocated and practiced love for the other and lost their lives for their efforts. Love and goodwill do not necessarily change an adversary or ensure one's safety.

Loving Without Reward

Some nonviolent peacemakers accept a false optimism that love will always triumph. They attempt to ground their opposition to violence on the premise that love does beget love, and love will be rewarded. These individuals tend to grow cynical or reject nonviolent peacemaking when they discover that conflict with another is not so simple or optimistic. Dale Brown grappled with the reality that one's love toward another often goes unreturned. Brown stated that he once possessed a belief that nonviolent peacemaking could change the world. He felt that nonviolent peacemaking was the means to elicit a similar loving response from the other. But his awareness of Hitler's Germany, the Hiroshima massacre, and the development of other totalitarian governments led him to question such an optimistic view of nonviolent peacemaking. The depth of evil is too firmly entrenched to be so quickly changed. Brown, like many other nonviolent peacemakers, found that love does not always produce the desired results.

> [Many nonviolent peacemakers] . . . when they met the hard realities of urban ghettos and the entrenched evil of power structure . . . discovered that pacifism provided no easy answers to the tough problems of our society.
>
> This skepticism was a part of my own pilgrimage. Like Soren Kierkegaard, I discovered that love does not always elicit a response of love. Love may even produce evil reactions. We hate a good, lov-

ing man, often because he shows us up for who and what we are. Jesus, whom we picture as the most loving man who ever lived, did not succeed in winning over his enemies. Instead, they hated him and nailed him to a cross.[2]

Brown contends that an individual cannot found his nonviolent peacemaking stance on the basis that love will always elicit love. If a nonviolent peacemaker accepts this idealistic approach, disillusion with others and nonviolent peacemaking is likely to follow.[3]

A. J. Muste articulated a similar theme — the nonviolent peacemaker cannot expect love to be returned. He contends that the ultimate vindication for the nonviolent peacemaker is the humble knowledge that she has not resorted to violence and hate, which can escalate the conflict. Muste says that the end result of any action cannot be guaranteed. The nation that goes to war cannot guarantee a victory. A rich man who has his house guarded by a private band of "protectors" cannot even guarantee his own safety. One of his own men may turn on him without warning. A. J. Muste states that nonviolent peacemaking, like all of life, offers no guarantee. The unpredictable nature of human existence forbids such a prophecy that love offered in the face of violence will always reap love. By offering love to another, one risks the possibility of failure and even death.[4]

Rollo May, in his work, *Power and Innocence: A Search for the Sources of Violence,* provides a helpful way of describing those who believe that love will always be returned. He describes an orientation to the world in which one's childhood is never released as pseudoinnocence; it is a fixation on the past, rather than a facing of the realities of the present. As a pseudoinnocent individual grows older, he still believes that he needs only to love another and the love will be returned.

> This type of [pseudo] innocence is a defense against having to confront the realities of . . . the war machine . . . status and prestige. . . . Innocence as a shield from responsibility is also a shield from growth. It protects us from new awareness and from identifying with the sufferings of mankind as well as with the joys, both of which are shut off from the pseudoinnocent person.[5]

Pseudoinnocence surrounds the human in daily living. For example, after the Nixon transcripts had been released, which clearly revealed Nixon's guilt, some individuals refused to believe that the President of the United States could be guilty of a crime. Their childhood image of the presidency would not accept the reality of a dishonest president. Some individuals did not even question why they had to serve in the military in Vietnam. Some men did not go to Vietnam because they believed in that war. They went to war simply because their country called for their services; they felt bound to answer affirmatively. They did not seriously question whether their government was right or wrong in its Southeast Asia campaign. A pseudoinnocent person follows orders without questioning the rightness of the command. Another example of pseudoinnocence is present in the cliché uttered in dramas and sometimes in real life: "I gave him everything he wanted, and now look at what he has done!" Clearly, just giving someone whatever they request does not ensure a similar response. Pseudoinnocence is an oversimplification of reality that attempts to escape personal responsibility by not challenging traditional childhood images, whether it be a person's perception of the government as always honest and correct in its foreign and domestic policy, or the adage that the human merely has to love the evil doer to elicit a loving response.

Individuals who promote nonviolent peacemaking under the optimistic assumption that love will always elicit a loving response, knowingly or unknowingly, accept the American myth of success. Many myths have emerged and disappeared since the nineteenth century, but the myth of success has continued to flourish. The rags-to-riches phenomenon is still a prevalent aspect of American culture. During the 1960s, Kennedy's New Frontier and Johnson's Great Society were manifestations of this myth of progress and success. During this time there was an optimism that the problems of the world were solvable by human ingenuity. However, during this reign of confidence, events sometimes pointed to an antithetical reality. Vietnam, Cambodia, Laos, and Cuba were places where violence was used to manipulate the will of foreign peoples. During the 1960s the myth of success was often blindly affirmed in the face of atrocity and human prejudice.

Not only the government, but a number of war protestors during the Vietnam years also displayed a belief in the myth of success. Many Vietnam protestors believed the system would change if people revealed a loving and nonviolent alternative. When the system did not quickly change, violence or apathy often became the option selected by pseudoinnocent nonviolent peacemakers. In relations with another the nonviolent peacemaker needs to recognize that a loving action may not elicit a similar response from his opponent. C. Wayne Zunkel's statement in an article, "Violence and Nonviolence," points to the movement from a pseudoinnocent understanding of peacemaking to a more realistic understanding of the human situation.

Contrary to the moving words of Dietrich Bonhoeffer, man

has not 'come of age.'. . . . Something of man has died. Like many
an adolescent, we have learned a little. But a little knowledge can be
a terrible thing. Suddenly we thought we were sufficient. But we are
not.[6]

A pseudoinnocent nonviolent peacemaking stance expects that love
and nonviolence will elicit a similar response from the other. The
strength of this stance is minimal, in that working for a peaceful and
just world for all people does not always ensure justice for oneself. A
pseudoinnocent peacemaking position is bound to promote disillusion
and frustration as a person discovers that a loving response often goes
unreciprocated.

The nonviolent peacemaker need not base her nonviolent peacemaking stance on the naive premise that love will always elicit a loving
response. She can ground her nonviolent peacemaking position in the
understanding that it may not be returned. This orientation allows an
individual to accept the world as often violent and work to change it,
without having undue expectations regarding the successfulness of his
efforts. One person stated that a nonviolent peacemaker must strive
for a more just and peaceful world, even though his dream may never
be attained. He stressed this view quite well in a humorous analogy
with a serious intent.

> I believe in peace, even though it seems like an elusive dream. I
> would rather chase a jack rabbit all over Iowa and not catch him
> than to chase a skunk half way around the block and catch him. I
> would rather go for the elusive dream of peace and fail than to go
> for the skunk of war, hatred and bloodshed and succeed.

To work for change without the assurance of reward points to accepting the possibility that a loving action may reap an antithetical
response.

Pitirim A. Sorokin states that love can stop aggressive interpersonal and intergroup conflict in about seventy to eighty-five percent of
the cases he studied. However, even by Sorokin's optimistic analysis,
it is possible that love will not be returned about one-fourth of the
time. Thus, the human must give love with the full knowledge that it
may not be returned. When love is offered in this realistic manner, an
individual does not use love to gain love for herself; she acts in love
because it is right. Sorokin contends that this unselfish, yet realistic
form of love has exerted the greatest and longest influence upon people and human history.

If we ask ourselves what sort of individuals have been more influential in human history, the answer is such individuals as Lao-Tze, Confucius, Moses, Guatama, Buddha, Mahavira, Jesus, St. Paul, St. Francis of Assisi, Mahatma Gandhi, and other founders of great religions, discoverers of eternal moral principles, and living incarnations of sublime, unselfish love. In contrast to the short-lived and mainly destructive influence of autocratic monarchs, military conquerers, revolutionary dictators, potentates of wealth, and other historical persons, these great apostles of spirituality and love have most tangibly affected the lives, minds, and bodies of untold millions, of many generations, during millennia of human history; and they are tangibly influencing us at the present time. They had neither army and arms nor physical force nor wealth nor any of the worldly means of influencing the historical destinies of nations. . . . And yet, together with a handful of their followers, they morally transformed millions of men and women, reshaped cultures and social institutions, and conditioned the course of history. They did all this by the mere power of their sublime, pure and overabundant love, by their unselfish spirituality and supreme wisdom.[7]

Sorokin's comments reveal the power of a realistic love based in the knowledge that an individual may not succeed in his efforts. The proponents of unselfish love committed themselves to what they considered right or truth. This realistic understanding of love is a form of authentic innocence, to use Rollo May's terminology. Authentic innocence is the innocence of the poet, artist, or anyone who preserves a feeling of awe and wonder about the world into adult life. However, as an authentically innocent individual maintains these attitudes in later life, a realistic perception of evil is not sacrificed.[8] An authentically innocent individual recognizes the violence that tends often to typify the human throughout the globe. As a nonviolent peacemaker accepts an authentically innocent view of the human experience, he offers the other a loving action without expecting a like response to necessarily be returned. The often violent nature of the world is acknowledged without supporting it by using violence to counter the present state of the human.

Authentic innocence is pointed to by Albert Camus in "Neither Victims Nor Executioners." He describes the importance of non-violent peacemaking, though it may not succeed. Camus points to the necessary element of authentic innocence; one engages in an action because it seems right, not because it will always be successful.

Over the expanse of five continents throughout the coming years an endless struggle is going to be pursued between violence and friendly persuasion, a struggle in which, granted, the former has a thousand times the chances of success than has the latter. But I have always held that, if he who bases his hope on human nature is a fool, he who gives up in the face of circumstances is a coward. And henceforth, the only honorable course will be to stake everything on a formidable gamble; that words are more powerful than munitions.[9]

An authentically innocent orientation to love accepts the realities of an evil world while still affirming the importance of nonviolent peacemaking in the struggle against violence and injustice.

Finding Meaning in Struggle

An authentically innocent individual accepts the possibility of suffering as one promotes nonviolent change in the status quo. To strive nonviolently for social justice requires a nonviolent peacemaker to ask the oppressed to forego violence in order not to legitimize the tactics of the oppressor. Encouraging the oppressed to accept a nonviolent stance is indeed a thankless position. Martin Luther King, Jr., as a proponent of nonviolent peacemaking, received the wrath of militant blacks and conservative whites. Jesus encountered a similar situation; he rejected both the way of the Zealots and the doctrine of the Pharisees. The extremes of violent revolution and the status quo were rejected by both Christ and Martin Luther King, Jr. They attempted to carve out a third alternative, nonviolent peacemaking, which resulted in criticism from the impatient and the content. The answer to violence is quite clear; a nonviolent peacemaker must suffer and possibly give her life in order to break the accumulative chain of violence and injustice.

John Howard Yoder, a Mennonite scholar, states that it is impossible to know the consequences of one's actions in advance. Thus, those who believe that a loving action will quickly change the world or elicit a loving response are taking upon themselves an impossible prediction. Yoder calls for a choice between the Kingdom of God and the kingdom of the earthly crown. He believes that the nonviolent peacemaker needs to reject the crown as Jesus did when he refused to become the Zealot leader.

> The choice that he [Jesus] made in rejecting the crown and accepting the cross was the commitment to such a degree of faithfulness to the character of divine love that he was willing for its sake to sacrifice 'effectiveness'. . . .
> What Jesus refers to in his call to cross-bearing is of . . . the inevitable suffering of those whose goal is to be faithful to that love that puts one at the mercy of one's neighbor.[10]

John Howard Yoder's emphasis of the radical separation between the Kingdom of God and the government is significant in that it points to the importance of authentic innocence, which recognizes the need for suffering. The difference between the Kingdom of God and the crown is that the former requires suffering through nonviolent means to invite a just and peaceful goal to emerge, and the latter requires suffering that will use virtually any means to achieve its predicted goal. An example of suffering in the affirmation of peace was provided by one individual. He said he could not remember when he did not believe that the way of militarism and crushing an opponent was ultimately self-defeating. During World War I, many of the men in his home church went to jail rather than participate in the war effort. They were offered alternative service positions, but during World War I those positions required an individual to wear a military uniform. Members of his home church saw the wearing of military garb as implicitly agreeing with the goals of the military establishment. In protest to the only alternative service option, many of the men in that peace church went to jail. They provided an example for the community. Also, these individuals accepted their suffering in incarceration as a necessary happening in their commitment to peace. The nonviolent peacemaker needs to question the rightness of actions, not just their effectiveness. The human can never predict the end result, but she does have some control over the means for attempting to fulfill a particular goal.

The pseudoinnocent individual is still caught in the quest for prediction as he attempts to elicit love with a loving action. He attempts to base actions on an unknowable prophecy, regarding the other's response. An authentically innocent nonviolent peacemaker may hope the other responds in a loving manner, but realizes that she cannot predict or dictate the response of the other. Thus, Jesus' rejection of the crown points to an authentic innocence that does not predict the response of the other; a loving action can be met by a violent response. The nonviolent peacemaker may even have to accept suffering in order to promote what she considers right.

The possibility of suffering as a consequence of the nonviolent peacemaking commitment was clearly recognized by representatives of the historic peace churches. One person stated that from a pragmatic viewpoint, nonviolent peacemaking may not be the best method of coping with violence; it may even cause suffering. This does not mean that suffering is invited or enjoyed; rather a nonviolent peacemaker needs to accept the fact that nonviolent actions may sometimes be met with violent responses of physical and psychological abuse. Thus, the traditional reward system of expecting a return on one's "investment" of nonviolent action and love toward the other is rejected. Jacques Ellul states:

> [Nonviolent peacemaking requires] Choosing different means, seeking another kind of victory, renouncing the marks of victory — this is the only possible way of breaking the chain of violence, of rupturing the circle of fear and hate.[11]

Dietrich Bonhoeffer illustrated a position of authentic innocence, which accepts the possibility of suffering. Although Bonhoeffer abdicated his nonviolent position in the face of Hitler's tyranny, his life and writings were based on the premise that a person often has to engage in self-sacrifice for his fellow humans. In his book, *Cost of Discipleship,* Bonhoeffer describes the difference between cheap and costly grace. Cheap grace is the ritualized forgiveness of one's sins without any change in one's behavior. For example, the pastor forgives all through a public prayer each Sunday; grace and forgiveness become mere words, rather than changes in one's life. But Bonhoeffer contends that costly grace requires a person to significantly alter his behavior and give himself to the following of Christ, even if suffering may result. Costly grace needs to be sought daily. Costly grace accepts self-suffering as a condition for discipleship.[12]

Cheap and costly grace can be correlated with pseudoinnocence and authentic innocence in nonviolent peacemaking, respectively. Pseudoinnocence is similar to cheap grace in that a person expects an easy movement toward change, in which kindness is rewarded with loving and accepting responses. Indeed, some individuals are quite naive about the long difficult task that is necessary to promote change.

Authentic innocence is similar to costly grace, in that the human accepts the fact that she may even lose her life in the act of caring for the other. Dietrich Bonhoeffer accepted an authentically innocent position as he protested against the Nazi regime. In 1939, he was on a lecture tour in the United States. He could have remained in the security of American borders, but he chose to return to Germany in order to protest Hitler's regime. This action cost Bonhoeffer his life. But he had accepted the possibility of his future fate before he returned to Germany. He realistically pursued the goal of a just world without naively expecting others to affirm his protest.

At the end of the section "The Last Days" in Bonhoeffer's *Letters and Papers from Prison* is the following poem:

He who punishes sin and willingly forgives,
God, I have loved this people.
That I carried its burdens
And seen its salvation — that is enough.
Keep me! Preserve me! My staff is sinking,
O faithful God, prepare my grave.[13]

These verses point to how a nonviolent peacemaker can gain a sense of significance or meaning in life, even in suffering. Meaning may be discovered as the human accepts suffering as sometimes necessary in the pursuit of a peaceful and just world. One individual pointed to this kind of meaning as resurrected life:

As I understand the New Testament, it calls a Christian to be so self-giving that he would lay down his own life. The cross and the resurrection are the primary themes of the New Testament. The ethics of the New Testament are derived out of these two emphases. The hope is that resurrection comes as a gift to those who participate in self-giving. . . . The theme of the resurrection permeates the New Testament at many levels. It means literally an after life and an understanding of meaning in the here and now. The one who gives himself is the one who experiences deliverance or meaning in his present life. Resurrection refers to a quality of life in the here and now as well as to an afterlife.

Thus, it is possible to find a meaning for one's existence, even in the midst of suffering, which may be unavoidable in the promoting of a peaceful and just world.

Viktor Frankl has attempted to describe how a person can gain meaning from uninvited suffering. In his own life, Frankl had to find meaning under the unbearable circumstances of Nazi concentration camps. Frankl stated that the individual who continued to struggle to live discovered a meaning for living. He even found meaning in the cross or suffering he had to endure. The captives attempted to carve out a meaning for life even in the midst of suffering, rather than deny their difficult situation with a false gesture of optimism.

[In] Nietzsche's words, 'He who has a *why* to live for can bear with almost any *how*'. . . . Woe to him who saw no more sense to his life, no aim, nor purpose, and therefore no point in carrying on. He was soon lost.[14]

Thomas Merton relates a story that summarizes the theme of authentic innocence, in which one finds meaning even in the face of suffering. On August 9, 1943, the German military authorities had

Austrian peasant Franz Jägerstätter beheaded. Jägerstätter was considered an enemy of the state, because he refused to participate in what he considered an "unjust war." He had clung to his contention that the war was unjust in the face of stern opposition from his friends, family, fellow Catholics, and the Catholic clergy. He was treated as a rebel and a traitor, and even accused of being too selfish to offer his life for the future welfare of his children. Jägerstätter could have escaped execution had he accepted a noncombatant position in the medical services. But he refused such an option because he felt it was an implicit admission that the Nazis were promoting a just war. After the execution of Franz Jägerstätter and the death of others committed to nonviolent approaches to the resolution of conflicting interests and ideologies, Thomas Merton wrote that the true heroes, in the eyes of most people, engaged in violent conflict. Merton indicated that suffering for violence is still affirmed by the general populace and suffering in nonviolent protest is seen as foolish and naive.[15] Indeed, to accept an authentically innocent nonviolent peacemaking position is to look for meaning in the rightness of one's actions, not in the reinforcing comments and actions of others.

The nonviolent peacemaker can find meaning even in the midst of suffering and violence. His purpose is a peaceful world, which requires both the means and goal to contribute to such a future project. Her actions may not be rewarded by others, but her life in the present may be enriched and made meaningful through her commitment to the project of peace. The depth of human evil which may promote suffering is accepted as a reality, while attempting to change the often violent nature of human life. The commitment and meaning in one's life is the reward of nonviolent peacemaking.

Part Two

Peacemaking Images in a Violent World

Chapter Four

The Roots of Violence

Human life is often based on assumptions of images regarding oneself and the other, rather than facts. The human is not totally knowable, due to the impossibility of accumulating all the necessary data about him. To a large extent, a person must rely on images of humans when she attempts to understand them. An image need not be factual in that it may not be experimentally or consensually validated. An image of the human directs a person's understanding of the other and himself. The importance of an image is not its correctness or validity, but its ability to structure an individual's view of the human. Without question, ". . . the image of the human person is a very basic part of any culture . . ."

Maurice Friedman, in his work *The Hidden Human Image*, believes that the human image can never be fully seen or understood; it can only be pointed to, but never fully uncovered. A good example of the hidden human image is the myth, in that it both reveals and obscures an understanding of the human. Academic and common theories regarding the person serve a similar function. The human is too complex to be described in any one particular theory. Each theory points to an image of the human and yet simultaneously hides as much, if not more, than it reveals.

> The human image, as I [Friedman] use the term, is not only an image of what man *is*, but also an image of authentic personal existence that helps him discover, in each age anew, what he may and can become, an image that helps him rediscover his humanity. 'Image' in this context means not a static picture but a meaningful, per-

sonal direction, a response from within to what one meets in each new situation, standing one's ground and meeting the world with the attitude that is rooted in this ground.[1]

Friedman's contention that an image gives personal direction or a way of viewing the other is also supported in a research document entitled *Changing Images of Man*. The goal of this manuscript was to describe different images of the human that have guided men's and women's actions in the past and views that may guide them in the future. *Changing Images of Man* revealed that each image of the human is selective. Some images are more narrow and others more comprehensive, but each is likely to both illuminate and obscure the image of the person. In short, the human image is illusive and cannot be totally grasped or understood.[2] A nonviolent peacemaker, like any other human, cannot know the other completely. She possesses only a partial view of the other. Yet this image is quite powerful; it directs her understanding of humans and actions toward others.

Human Destructiveness

A number of the representatives of the historical peace churches articulated an image of the human as essentially evil. One peacemaker stated that throughout the years he had come to believe in the concept of original sin. He found himself close to the apostle Paul, in that the things he wanted to do he didn't do, and the things he didn't want to do he found himself doing. Another person said he had never doubted the doctrine of original sin, because there is so much evidence for it.

> Man is inherently aggressive. His survival as a species depended on
> it before the onset of the age of technology. His aggression as a
> primitive was directed toward plants and other animals as objects of
> food, clothing, and shelter and sometimes his fellow men. . .

One individual said he believed in the doctrine of original sin, in that an infant is born into a corrupt world and is quickly influenced by it. These statements reflect a common theme that is prevalent in many people's image of the human—humankind has a natural tendency for evil or choosing alternatives that may produce destructive results. A number of conflict theorists have postulated similar thoughts concerning the tendency of the human to engage in evil or destructive acts of aggression.

Erich Fromm finds it interesting that so much attention is presently being paid to the realities of violence and destruction. Volumes of theoretical speculation on the nature of conflict and aggression are now being popularized. Fromm does not consider this preoccupation with aggression surprising; however, he does find the ignoring and/or ignorance of Freud's work on this matter disheartening. The public still equates Freud with the life instinct or sexuality. Yet, in the 1920s, Sigmund Freud formulated a theory in which the "death instinct" or passion to destroy was given equal strength to the passion to live.[3] As Freud postulated the dichotomy of the life instincts and death instincts, he carefully studied the phenomenon of human aggression. He contended that the death instinct was either directed toward the organism itself in an act of self-destruction or was directed toward others in an effort to destroy them rather than oneself.

> Even though Freud suggested at various times that the power of the death instinct can be reduced the basic assumption remained: man was under the sway of an impulse to destroy either himself or others, and he could do little to escape this tragic alternative. It follows that, from the position of the death instinct, aggression was not essentially a reaction to a stimuli but a constant flowing impulse rooted in the constitution of the human organism.[4]

Fromm considers Freud's postulation of a free flowing aggressive impulse that periodically requires reduction as a major limitation to the understanding of human aggression. Freud was led to this view of aggression when he embraced the principle of tension reduction. Freud's assertion that a person is motivated by tension reduction is too simplistic. Tension increase as well as tension decrease tend to propel human actions. Fromm contends that Freud was committed to the axiom of tension reduction because he was impressed by the physiological theories of his teachers, rather than witnessing such happenings in his clinical practice.[5] With his emphasis on tension reduction, Freud announced an image that reveals the human as having to release aggressive energy that accumulated with or without a reaction to aversive stimuli. The human is destined to be aggressive and to seek release of that energy.

Ultimately, Sigmund Freud did not foresee a glorious future for humans unless they learned to sublimate their aggressive impulses. As he wrote in 1930 and 1931 and the power and menace of Hitler was starting to loom as the emergence of the demonic, he was not optimistic about the human's future possibilities.

> . . . I can offer them no consolation. . . . Men have gained control over the forces of nature to such an extent that with their help they would have no difficulty in exterminating one another to the very last man. They know this, and hence comes a large part of their current unrest, their unhappiness and their mood of anxiety. And

now it is to be expected that the other of the two "Heavenly Powers," eternal Eros, will make an effort to assert himself in the struggle with his equally immortal adversary. But who can foresee with what success and with what result?[6]

Even though Freud spoke of the life instinct and said that aggression could be reduced through sublimation, one fact regarding his theory of aggression looms even more significant—human beings are under the sway of a tragic impulse, to destroy themselves or others. And there is no escape from this vicious cycle of aggression. Aggression is not a reaction to stimuli, but a constant flow of impulses rooted in the very constitution of the human. Sigmund Freud points to the death instinct as the evil that typifies the human.

Current literature on the problem of human aggression accepts many of the fundamental premises promoted by Sigmund Freud with even greater emphasis on the destructive characteristics of the human. Konrad Lorenz accepts a tension reduction or hydraulic understanding of aggression. The human can withstand a certain degree of aggressive feeling, but as these feelings build up they must eventually be released. Like Freud, Lorenz considers human aggression an instinct that is constantly energized by an ever flowing source of energy. Once the aggressive energy accumulates to a sufficient level, an explosion will occur, with or without the aid of an initiator or stimulus. When finally released, the dammed-up aggression may lead to cruelty and killing, according to Lorenz. But Lorenz also considers this aggression a positive element in that humans for years have needed this aggressive instinct to protect themselves in order to survive.

The problem that Lorenz now visualizes is that the human has become so technologically sophisticated that aggressive instincts, which are bound to periodically emerge, can now do much greater harm then ever before. Mechanized society has provided an atmosphere for socially acceptable forms of competition that are based in an aggressive orientation that seeks to destroy the opponent. For example, a businessman may not be satisfied to have enough customers to support his own business; he would rather eliminate his competition, in order to be the sole arbitrator of price.

The positive aspects of aggression are now turning into the monstrous possibilities for the destruction of the human ecological system. Konrad Lorenz articulates this theme quite strongly in his work *On Aggression*. He states that animals possess inhibitions which control their aggression, by preventing them from harming or destroying members of their own species. Lorenz says that inhibitory mechanisms are strongest and most highly differentiated in predator animals that possess the potential of killing creatures of their own species. Animals which are not predators but are often chased by other animals, are usually not a threat to their own species. Thus, these animals have developed little, if any, inhibitory mechanisms to discourage killing members of their own species.

Lorenz goes on to say that the human as a non-predatory creature has inherited few inhibitory mechanisms for aggression. And now whatever inhibitory mechanisms an individual does have are often inoperative, because much of modern warfare is carried on with "remote-control" weapons that allow one to distance oneself from one's prey. The technologically sophisticated weaponry can cause danger and harm that was never before possible for the human to inflict. According to Lorenz, human aggression was necessary for protection and the gathering of food in the early stages of the evolutionary process. This aggression did not need an inhibitory mechanism, because the human was not capable of killing large numbers of his own species. But the advent of sophisticated technological weaponry and the lack of inhibitory mechanisms have led to a demonic nightmare, where the human is now capable of eliminating human life as it is now recognized.[7]

Freud and Lorenz both see the human as having the potential of exploding into aggressive behavior without a stimulus to promote such an action. Neither theorist sees the human as having the ability to adequately control aggression. It is this bleak aggressive thesis that Robert Ardrey promotes even more avidly. He describes the findings of Raymond Dart, who provided a startling explanation of the taungs skull in 1924. Dart believed that this infant skull found in Africa was that of a creature halfway between human and gorilla. He projected that such a creature as an adult must have been four feet tall, stood erect, had a brain the size of a gorilla's and from the creature's teeth determined that it must have been carnivorous. This creature, *Australopithecus africanus*, was considered a transitional being who possessed all the qualities of the human species except the same size brain. But during the 1920s, the scientific community was still convinced that human life had arisen in Asia, not in Africa. Thus, people were quite dubious of Dart's assertions.

Undaunted by criticism, Dart continued his effort to prove the validity of his contentions. So unyielding was Dart's conviction that Robert Broom, a seventy-year-old zoologist of world acclaim, emerged from retirement to search for more conclusive evidence to Dart's contentions. In 1936, Broom located a cave near Johannesburg, South Africa, which contained the skull, brain case, and teeth of an adult australopithecine. This discovery confirmed the projection that Dart had made earlier. Subsequent discoveries at five different South African sites confirmed Dart's original hypothesis regarding the existence and size of an adult australopithecine. Then in 1949, Raymond Dart made another statement that startled the anthropological world.

> . . . [Dart] published a paper in the *American Journal of Physical Anthropology* claiming that *Australopithecus africanus* had gone armed. Study of some fifty-odd baboon skulls from various sites associated with the southern ape had revealed a curious, characteristic double depression. Dart concluded that the baboons had met sudden death at the hands of the southern ape; that the man-ape had used a weapon and that his favourite weapon had been the antelope humerous bone.
>
> The use of weapons had preceded man.[8]

According to Ardrey, Dart proposed one major thesis with his conclusion about the murderous tactics of *Australopithecus africanus*. The human was only able to evolve out of his anthropoid background because he was a killer. Ardrey accepts Dart's assertion that the human evolved out of a killer background. He believes that humans survived because they were adept at using weapons to a strategic advantage. Ardrey ends *African Genesis* with a commentary on the aggressive state of the human which cannot be forgotten or ignored. "*Australopithecus africanus* lies buried not in limey caves, but in my heart and your heart. . . We are Cain's children, all of us."[9]

Many individuals do not accept the assumption that the human is necessarily in the direct line of evolution with *Australopithecus africanus*. Other scholars are not even sure if they can accept the fact that *Australopithecus africanus* actually used tools for killing or not; possibly tools were utilized for cutting and pounding inanimate objects only. But whether or not an individual accepts the assumption or theoretical positions suggested by Ardrey, the fact that the human does murder fellow human beings is undeniable. Thus, people who contend that humans are prone to engage in destructive actions are theoretically supported in their assertions. The human is quite capable of violent and evil action toward the other. An image of the human as evil does point to an undeniable part of the human life—that man and woman throughout the centuries have taken the lives of other human beings.

The Person as Innately Good?

A number of the representatives of the historical peace churches visualized the human as primarily good. One peacemaker with a psychology background stated that his reading of Maslow and Rogers had led him to see the human as basically good. He did not see the world as inherently violent. The goodness of the person is often covered by violent responses. Constructive potentials only need to be allowed to surface. Another individual stated that the human is inherently good and attempts to constantly strive for what is right. A number of the responses revealed an understanding of the human as somewhat good, but definitely not predominately evil. "I certainly do not feel that man is inherently evil. I would like to feel that man is inherently good, and I come close to subscribing to the idea that everyone wants his own growth . . ." Another individual said that the human is born good and the evil that she manifests she is driven to commit. The goodness of the other may be hidden beneath layers of defensive and destructive attitudes and actions. But there is an inner core of goodness in each person that can emerge with support and encouragement. It is this inner core of goodness that individuals in the third force or humanistic psychology attempt to uncover in their clients.

Carl Rogers, the founder of client-centered therapy, has emphasized throughout his long and distinguished career the innate goodness of the human. Rogers postulates that each human organism from the moment of birth to the inevitable end possesses an innate motivational force, the tendency toward constructive actualization of his human potentialities. Carl Rogers believes that the human needs to allow her inborn goodness to emerge in order to actualize her potential. However, individuals are seldom able to actualize themselves to the fullest extent. The human introjects the values of others to obtain positive self-regard and the acceptance of others. For example, a salesman may feel he needs to take a potential buyer out to lunch and order alcoholic drinks. In order to please his clients, the salesman may consume too much alcohol too often. His innate actualizing tendency may relay messages that he should stop this sales practice, but his need for positive self-regard and fear of his clients rejecting him leads to abuse of alcohol. Rogers contends that much of life involves meeting the expectations of others, rather than following one's own actualizing tendencies. Client-centered therapy attempts to provide an atmosphere where the client can begin to follow her inner motivational force and forego the need to introject the values of others.

Through his years of clinical practice with confused and distraught persons, Rogers has become convinced that if individuals follow their own innate or organismic valuing process, then constructive and socially beneficial choices will result or follow. Client-centered therapy as promoted by Carl Rogers is optimistic about the human person, as long as he can avoid the tendency to introject the values of others. Rogers attempts to provide an atmosphere where a person can reject external pressures to conform and follow her own actualizing tendency.

Carl Rogers is joined by Abraham Maslow in that both men are concerned with humans uncovering their self-actualizing tendencies. Maslow, who is often referred to as the father of third-force or humanistic psychology, considers the human as inherently good, or at least neutral. Maslow is not fearful of the inner core of the human being. He is content to allow the individual's inner self to emerge.

> Human nature is not nearly as bad as it has been thought to be. In fact it can be said that the possibilities of human nature have customarily been sold short.
> Since this inner nature is good or neutral rather than bad, it is best to bring it out and to encourage it rather than suppress it. If it is permitted to guide our lives, we grow healthy, fruitful, and happy.[10]

Abraham Maslow has attempted to describe the inner core of the human that has constructive impulses and strives for fulfillment. Maslow believes that the human organism possesses biological wisdom that promotes self-governing, self-choosing and autonomous behavior. Due to the constructive nature of a person's inner foundation, Abraham Maslow advocates a Taoistic counseling style. In Taoistic counseling, the counselor makes a conscious effort:

> . . . not to impose his will upon the patient, but rather to help the patient . . . discover what is inside him, the patient. The psychotherapist helps him to discover what he wants or desires, what is good for him, the patient, rather than what is good for the therapist. This is the opposite of controlling, propagandizing, molding, teaching in the old sense.[11]

Abraham Maslow refers to Taoistic therapy that allows the individual's inner self to emerge, as an uncovering. He contends that each individual can uncover his innate drive toward self-actualization and constructive impulses, through a Taoistic Therapeutic process.

Both Rogers and Maslow emphasize the goodness of human beings who can reject introjected values and uncover their actualizing tendencies. Their faith in the human being propels them to see no one as inherently evil; only the constructive impulses have been stilted and covered over. Rogers and Maslow base their understanding of the person on the premise that to care for another allows her to feel safe enough to explore her inner self, which is composed of a constructive inner core. This humanistic mode of counseling expresses a sincere caring for the other, that is not paternalistic nor superficial. Rather, it is an unconditional respect for the individual. The individuality and separateness of the person is recognized and accepted. There is a sincere desire to aid the person in his quest to achieve more meaning and satisfaction from life. Thus, these two therapeutic systems work on the assumption that care for people can allow constructive impulses to emerge and to begin to direct their behavior.

Inviting Good — Understanding Evil

The preceding material pointed to the destructive and constructive impulses of the human. The importance of these images is that they reveal the dual nature of the human predicament — the human has almost infinite capacities for both good and evil. One peace church member said, "I think the human being is both good and bad. . . . His finiteness leads him to fight to survive. Yet, he is often able to transcend his lower nature." Another individual said he too saw the human person as a combination of both good and evil. The Friends' (Quakers') concept of the inner light made a lot of sense to him, in that the inner light is the ideal in the midst of evil. He believed there is an inner light in every person, which corresponds to a reverence for life. Thus, the recognition of evil is mitigated by recognition of the inner light in every person. Viktor Frankl summarizes the human's dual nature in the closing pages of *Man's Search for Meaning,* which describes his own experiences in Nazi concentration camps.

> In concentration camps . . . we watched and witnessed some of our comrades behave like swine while others behaved like saints. Man has both potentialities within himself. . . . Our generation is realistic, for we have come to know man as he really is. After all, man is the being who has invented the gas chambers of Auschwitz; however, he is also that being who has entered those gas chambers upright, with the Lord's Prayer or the *Shema Yisrael* on his lips.[12]

Nonviolent peacemaking can incorporate the learnings from Freud, Lorenz, and Ardrey, as well as Rogers, Maslow and the humanistic movement. A nonviolent peacemaker needs to accept the reality of violence while allowing and inviting the goodness of others to unfold by caring for them. Thus, this chapter points to an image of the human as both good and evil, in which the nonviolent peacemaker works to elicit the constructive impulses from the other with full knowledge that a destructive response may or may not result. The nonviolent peacemaker invites the goodness of the other to emerge, even in conflict and confrontation, but is not shocked or surprised when an antithetical response is the answer. This manner of dealing with the human's dual potentialities is summarized by the following comment.

> . . . I have a kind of basic faith in the goodness of humanity, and that it can be called forth and responded to, but I'm never surprised when a person acts in another way. I always hope for and expect that they can act one way [constructively], but I'm never surprised when they act another.

Martin Luther King, Jr. articulated a similar theme, in which he described his understanding of human nature. He said that the human is neither full of inherent goodness that liberalism promotes nor condemned as always evil like the neo-orthodoxy suggests. "An adequate understanding of man is found neither in the thesis of liberalism nor the antithesis of neo-orthodoxy, but in a synthesis that reconciles the truths of both."[13] The necessary synthesis for the nonviolent peacemaker involves accepting the possibility of violence while attempting to elicit good from the other with full knowledge that an antithetical response may occur.

Chapter Five

The Inevitable Conflict

Unfortunately, people who affirm the importance of a nonviolent peacemaking stance may sometimes equate human conflict with interpersonal violence. Whether knowingly or unknowingly, some nonviolent peacemakers have an image of peace that entails no conflict. Thus, conflict is sometimes viewed as an evil in which a person should not engage. One peacemaker related his honest difficulty in accepting the need for human conflict. He had to struggle to accept conflict happenings that may promote needed clarification and understanding of issues between persons. But his years of teaching led him to recognize the positive possibilities of conflict. Another person stated that some religiously based nonviolent peacemakers traditionally tend to smooth over conflict in family, organizations, and institutions. They do not confront conflict. One peacemaker contended that many nonviolent peacemaking sermons over the years have emphasized the suffering servant and turning the other cheek scriptural references. Jesus' confrontations with the Pharisees have not been emphasized as much. In family and organizations, pent-up emotions and anger have occurred because of the difficulty of accepting conflict as compatible with nonviolent peacemaking. In the Peace Corps, this individual worked with people who openly confronted conflict, but in a caring fashion. At that point, he came to see that nonviolent peacemaking meant working through conflict, not just avoiding it.

One representative of the historic peace churches discussed the problem of conflict avoidance. He stated that a nonviolent peacemaker is concerned about the limited benefits of coercion. The nonviolent peacemaker is aware that as a person acts out of expediency the results are often not lasting. But this knowledge is often mistranslated by many nonviolent peacemakers to mean that nonconflict and acquiescence is the correct response to coercion. Often peacemaking requires a prophetic stance, which entails the possibility of being misunderstood. The nonviolent peacemaker needs to accept the conflict and animosity that may result from taking this position. Even though conflict is painful when it occurs, it may bring a community closer together and open channels for better communication in the long run. One individual stated that it did not please him when conflict arose, but he did attempt to deal with it to the best of his abilities. Yet another peacemaker said that conflict must be dealt with, but he hoped that he would never begin to enjoy the conflict process.

The Positive Possibilities of Conflict

Conflict is seldom viewed as an enjoyable process by nonviolent peacemakers; yet, they recognize that conflict can have positive possibilities. This points to the notion that conflict is not always a destructive happening. Conflict is often necessary to clarify issues and concerns. To always avoid conflict eliminates the possibility for new insight and understanding that the conflicting situation may reveal. One person affirmed the need for the human conflict in order to clarify concerns and generate necessary discussion.

> I find myself in a fairly high level of conflict in this college setting, with a whole series of people. And it's usually not personal. I'm fairly conflictless in terms of interpersonal relations. But on the question of public policy and procedure and so on, I find myself frequently running a kind of conflict situation. I tend to think that's creative. I tend to think that social settings tend to be protective of themselves and that it's conflict that chases out, gets things out front that need to be out front. So I don't find that bad. I've been influenced to some degree by the school of thought which is related to Harold Laski, who argues that the idea behind democracy is conflict, that democracy is a way by which to regularize conflict, but it's not inherently anticonflict. That is, they view this conflict as a kind of motor to get things going.

Another individual said he wanted to affirm conflict. It can strengthen people and encourage them to grow. Yet another peacemaker stated, " . . . I think it's possible for an outsider to look at a conflict situation and say that it is destructive, when actually the participants may grow together and stronger in the process. Conflict between humans can generate positive consequences that may go undiscovered without open disagreement.

The above comments describe conflict as potentially helpful and constructive. The presence of conflict may reveal a healthy, not a destructive relationship. The absence of conflict between opposing parties may indicate that some form of physical or psychological violence is being exerted in order to repress differences. Sometimes families, groups, or governments attempt to repress conflict in the public domain, but this action does not make a problem or concern disappear. Instead, secretive meetings and unexpressed feelings of resentment become the by-products of not dealing openly with conflicting interests. Kenneth Boulding, the Quaker economist and peace researcher, has stated that the "chronic disease of society" is the equating of conflict and violence. Society can then legitimize using increased violence in order to repress conflict. Whenever conflict arises, it is quickly brought under control by a show of force. This response to conflict is typified by the presence of the National Guard at Kent State University or the parent or authority who states, "You must do as I say, because I said it and for no other reason." In either case, the result is the same—conflict is repressed, not dealt with in a constructive manner. Boulding has stated that a violent response to conflict:

> ' . . . frequently inhibits settlement; for it leaves no path to settlement open but conquest, and this may not be possible.' Short of complete annihilation, Boulding asserts, violence is able to end conflict by repressing it, driving it underground, but it can do so only as long as it remains preponderant on the side of the victor. Such resolution as may occur must come from another quarter. Violence cannot affect it.[1]

An atmosphere without conflict is not always an indication of a healthy situation; it may be a sign of repression due to physical or psychological violence.

In America, the conflict between black and white was repressed for years through psychological and physical violence. Blacks were kept "in their place" and not granted the rights and freedoms of white Americans. Segregated schools, churches and rest rooms, literacy tests before voting in the South, and placement in the back seats of public transportation were but a few of the ways the conflict was repressed. As long as the black people were held in check with these measures, the conflict only simmered below the surface. In 1954, Martin Luther King, Jr., then a pastor in Montgomery, Alabama, aided the black people in nonviolent protest and resistance. A bus boycott was enacted that established massive noncooperation and a desire to ride the buses in dignity, rather than humiliation. And so began an intensive nonviolent campaign to reclaim the dignity of the black people.

King did not promote violence but he did encourage needed conflict. As William Puffenberger stated, " . . . one of the great things about the techniques used by Martin Luther King, Jr. was his way of escalating the conflict but not escalating the violence." Martin Luther King, Jr. realized that violence repressed conflict and that in order for change to occur, conflict would have to surface. The white community would have to face the repressed tension and conflict between the races. The fact that human conflict can be destructive is undeniable, but not all conflict should be avoided. Conflict escalation without accompanying violence allows issues to be dealt with that may have been previously ignored.

In her edited work, *Peacemaking: A Guide to Conflict Resolution for Individuals, Groups, and Nations,* Barbara Stanford has attempted to reinforce the notion that conflict is not necessarily destructive and is an inevitable part of human existence. She contends that conflict is often associated with lack of peace. However, Stanford believes that the elimination of conflict may lead to disastrous results.

> Conflict is so central to life that it cannot be eliminated without eliminating life as we know it. . . . A peace achieved by eliminating conflict is the peace of the graveyard. . . .
>
> Peacemaking, then, does not require eliminating conflict; instead, it requires effectively handling and resolving conflicts.[2]

Conflict in interpersonal encounters is not only an inevitable element of human communication, but it can actually enhance a relationship. Conflict happens when dissimilar perceptions, ideologies, values or desires collide. Conflict can enhance a conversation or relationship as an opponent offers her view of a situation. In conflict, new ideas or new possibilities for viewing an activity may be opened to both parties. A relationship can quickly grow static and boring if each party is continually in agreement with the other. Ideally, each human relationship should manifest an optimal level of difference in which there is just enough dissimilarity to maintain interest without attempting to verbally destroy the other. Not only is conflict inevitable, it is essential to the maintenance of a healthy, growing, and interesting human relationship.

Some positive aspects of interpersonal conflict are also described by Richard Walton in *Interpersonal Peacemaking: Confrontations and Third Party Consultation.* Walton states that a moderate level of conflict may have the following helpful consequences: First, it may allow new motivation and energy to be discovered by the conflicting parties. Second, the innovation of individuals may be heightened due to a perceived necessity to deal with the conflict. Third, each individual in the conflict situation can develop an increased understanding of his own perceptions by having to articulate his views in a conflicting and argumentative situation. Fourth, each person often develops a firmer sense of identity; conflict allows values and belief systems to emerge into fuller view.[3] Bach and Wyden in *The Intimate Enemy: How to Fight Fair in Love and Marriage,* attempt to teach couples the rules for constructive and beneficial conflict. They contend that, "verbal conflict between intimates is not only acceptable, especially between husbands and wives; it is constructive and highly desirable."[4]

An example of the positive, but nevertheless difficult process of meeting a conflict situation is revealed in the following incident. An organization was having a major conflict over the abilities of one staff member. Some members accused this particular individual of incompetence. But when the accusers were asked who had ever shared negative comments with them about this staff member, only vague antecedents such as "they" or "a number of committed persons" were given. This process of criticism went on for about one year. The staff person under question offered no protest to the accusations. He simply sat back and allowed the criticism to mushroom and become distorted. Due to the staff member's decision not to confront accusations, other members began to doubt his ability to contribute a positive force to the organization. Comments such as, "He is incompetent," or "He is always in a fog," became estimates of the staff member's ability. Finally, the staff member began to challenge his accusers. He documented his sixty-hour work week and the large number of projects in which he was engaged. He then pushed his accusers for specifics, rather than general statements of criticism. He finally entered the conflict with those members that questioned his abilities.

The result of both parties grappling with the conflict was that fundamental issues of disagreement, rather than vague generalities regarding this staff member's ability, began to surface. Two significant happenings can be attributed to the conflict situation: (1) individuals clarified their concerns—the staff member was not assertive enough in his work, and (2) the staff member displayed late in the conflict situation that he could assert himself as a viable promoter of something he believed. Conflict opened the door for clarification of issues and potentially for reconciliation as the issues and demands on the staff member were made more explicit.

Peacemaking — A Lonely Affirmation

Even with the knowledge that conflict can be a positive process, there is often loneliness as a person takes an unpopular stand. One interviewee stated that whenever an individual supports a minority position, such as nonviolent peacemaking, one will encounter the problem of loneliness. The loneliness of a nonviolent peacemaker's stance is described quite clearly in a paraphrase of one peacemaker's comments. When he first made his stand as a nonviolent peacemaker, he was discriminated against by his home community. After he had declared his position as a conscientious objector, some of his friends would not even acknowledge him. When he was in a small community in alternative service, he again experienced discrimination. Store clerks in the community would not even serve a conscientious objector. This nonviolent peacemaker had to learn to deal with loneliness; the stand he affirmed placed him in opposition to the mainstream of the World War II social structure. The conscientious objector's position on violence led him to experience conflict with others. It is this conflict that an individual experiences when he opposes the status quo that often leaves him feeling isolated and alone in personal beliefs.

Charles Chatfield relates the story of a conscientious objector during World War I. Harold Gray was given a noncombatant position, but he was still drafted as a part of the armed services. On numerous occasions he was given chores and duties that he felt contributed to the military effort. When this occurred, he refused to aid the military in their requests. He used hunger strikes and acts of noncooperation to emphasize his disagreement and noncompliance with the military establishment. Chatfield refers to Gray's efforts as "a lonely affirmation" of his principles of peace. Conflict was generated throughout Harold Gray's military noncombatant tenture, but he struggled to affirm the values he cherished. Gray must have realized the loneliness of his commitment most pointedly when he was finally released from his duties. Harold Gray's reward was stamped on his discharge papers: "'. . . character bad.'"[5] Gray must have often felt that he was opposing a force that was much too anonymous and frightening for one man to change. Chatfield states that other peacemakers such as Harold Gray received little support from the populace during World War I.

> [Yet] . . . the objectors asserted that pacifism was a duty for which they were willing to suffer. At the very least they were 'pleading for the social value of heresy.' If the will of the nation is truly the ultimate ethical authority, then pacifists were but a 'slightly bedraggled fringe on the robe of Mars.' But if men owe their first allegiance to anything other than public opinion, then conscientious

objection was an important affirmation of that duty.
For many it was a lonely affirmation.[6]

In the early 1700s, a Brethren leader and minister, John Naas, had to make a lonely decision that could have cost him his life. John Naas was known for a number of unusual qualities. He was described a half century after his death as an "incomparable teacher," and his ministry was greatly appreciated by those who knew of him. But John Naas had another unusual characteristic—he was quite tall and possessed great physical strength. Thus, as the Prussian King searched for men he regarded suitable for military training, he was attracted to this large and powerful man. Naas refused to join the King's army, because he wanted to be true to his Lord's commandment, "Thou shalt not kill." The King's officers then attempted to persuade John Naas to change his stand by torturing him. "The torture consisted of pinching, thumb-screwing, and finally hanging by the great toe and left thumb. Despite these humiliating and painful treatments he remained faithful, and the officers cut him down fearing his death."[7] John Naas was finally brought before the King of Prussia where he explained that his allegiance was first to the "Prince of Peace." The King so admired the courage of this man that he actually commended him and sent him on his way with a gold coin as a gift.

A nonviolent peacemaker who is attempting to work for social change or to stand fast to her own belief may have to make solitary decisions that can promote animosity or even threaten her life. The following story regarding John Kline again stresses this theme. John Kline was a Brethren physician who lived in the South during the 1800s. He opposed the Confederate cause in the war and had refused to serve in the Confederate army, due to his commitment to peace and the sanctity of human life. John Kline was also committed to his peace church; thus he insisted on going to the Brethren Annual meetings, even when he had to cross from southern to northern territory. In 1862, he safely left the southern stronghold in Virginia and traveled to Ohio; fortunately he was able to return to Virginia without harm after the Annual Meeting had concluded. However, in 1863, traveling across southern and northern boundaries had become even more dangerous. Brethren in Virginia attempted to persuade John Kline to remain home and not attend the Annual Meeting in Pennsylvania. But John Kline felt he could not heed the advice of his fellow Brethren, so once again he attended the Annual Meeting at the risk of his own life.

John Kline's presence at the Annual Meetings helped maintain a unity between the southern and northern based Brethren. He was an outstanding leader and had been the moderator of the Annual Meeting in 1860. Because of his constant crossing into the northern states to attend his church's Annual Meetings, John Kline was viewed as a northern sympathizer or possibly even a northern spy. He was also quite unpopular because he treated the wounds of southern deserters. Throughout this time of tension between the North and South, John Kline was aware that his own personal actions were causing much conflict between southern loyalists and himself. He told his fellow Brethren at the Annual Meeting in Indiana:

> 'Possibly you may never see my face or hear my voice again. I am now on my way back to Virginia, not knowing the things that befall me there. It may be that bonds and afflictions abide me. But I feel that I have done nothing worthy of bonds or of death; and none of these things move me; neither count I my life dear unto myself, so that I may finish my course with joy . . . '[8]

John Kline did not shrink from what he perceived to be his duty, even as it became apparent that the conflict and animosity he was generating between himself and a number of Confederates might cost him his life. Then on June 15, 1864, a group of Confederate soldiers were given the authority to silence those who appeared to be Union sympathizers.

> As John Kline rode along the way he had said he would go—across Howdyshell Ridge—the soldier who had been selected to fire the shot raised his gun to fire, but then lowered it saying, 'I can't shoot that man.' His partner grumbled, 'You're no soldier,' and stepping out of the bushes, fired point blank at Kline's back. Then, stepping forward, he fired a second shot into the fallen man's breast to make certain that the deed had been fulfilled. . . .
> Immediately, the soldiers disappeared into the heavily wooded area from which they had ambushed Kline. . . . He was carrying some money and a watch, but he had not been robbed; obviously, money was not the motivation in the murder.[9]

John Kline was assassinated because he had promoted too much conflict for others to tolerate. He did not attempt to avoid his role as a conflict initiator, nor did he consciously work to create conflict. The solitary decisions that John Kline had to make regarding the carrying out of his belief system had cost him his life. His decisions had placed him in conflict with those who oppressed and violated others.

To be a prophetic voice in an often violent society, the nonviolent peacemaker may need to stand as a solitary figure attempting to change the ways of the majority. Martin Buber was particularly impressed by Gandhi's desire to stand for a truth even as others disagreed with his perception. In February of 1922, the All-India Committee attempted to force Gandhi to take the words "nonviolent" and "truthful" out of the program statement. To that challenge Gandhi remarked:

> 'If I stood before the prospect of finding myself in a minority of *one* voice, I humbly believe that I would have the courage to remain in such a hopeless minority. This is for me the only truthful position.'[10]

Gandhi points to a courage to stand in the face of conflict without yielding to that which one considers to be the wrong or untruthful alternative.

The shirking of responsibility or the shifting of blame to higher authorities is unfortunately a much more prevalent response to human conflict than the stance of a Gandhi. It is often easier to obey an authority or even a peer than to announce a minority or solitary opinion. One of the most well known experiments that is used to demonstrate the high level of obedience that individuals accept was conducted by Stanley Milgram at Yale University. Milgram set up an experiment where subjects were to use electric shock treatments to force another to learn more quickly. The person given the responsibility of administering the shocks was always a naive subject, but the person who *feigned* being shocked was an accomplice of Milgram's. When the accomplice made an error, the subject would administer higher and higher voltages to increase the "learning." In reality, the accomplice received no electric shock, but he behaved as if he did. As the accomplice screamed for compassion, sixty-five per cent of the subjects went beyond the 300 volt maximum shock level. The results of Milgram's study are frightening. Milgram's experiment points dramatically to the notion that the human is quite capable of obediently following orders to the detriment of his fellows.

However, the Milgram study also has an encouraging aspect that is seldom emphasized. Thirty-five percent of the participants refused to follow Milgram's orders to the final climax. And even those subjects who did complete the task did so with great reluctance.

> The main result of Milgram's study seems to be one he does not stress: the presence of conscience in most subjects, and their pain when obedience made them act against their conscience. Thus, while the experiment can be interpreted as another proof of the easy dehumanization of man, the subjects' reactions show rather the contrary—the presence of intense forces within them that find cruel

behavior intolerable.[11]

The results of Milgram's study suggest that people can raise their voices against the ongoing happenings. For nonviolent peacemakers, it may be necessary to raise their solitary voices to challenge assumptions that may otherwise go untried, even if conflict is uncovered in the process.

The difficulty of affirming one's beliefs in the midst of disagreement and conflict cannot be minimized. But it seems that the human may have to take that lonely stand to be responsible to his own belief for a more just and peaceful world. This loneliness in the face of conflict can be viewed as a test that the initiator of change must bear. Martin Buber contended that sometimes " . . . man finds the truth to be true only when he stands its test. Human truth is here bound up with the responsibility of the person."[12] An individual's understanding of what is true and just may put him in conflict with his fellows and require him to become a solitary voice announcing a need for peace and justice.

Chapter Six

Caring—An Act of Power

A nonviolent peacemaker's belief system may naturally lead him into conflict situations, as the previous section revealed. When a nonviolent peacemaker enters conflict, she rejects violence as a method for dealing with it. Richard Gregg contends that violent struggle only represses the concerns and energy of the dominated party. Sooner or later the repressed emotional energy will be used in an act of revenge or retaliation. Gregg also considers it psychologically unhealthy to repress one's own emotions. Gregg believes that a human cannot remain passive when oppression appears; often direct action is the only healthy outlet for a person's emotional energy.

> Problems of conflict cannot, however, always be solved by firm refusals, kindly spirit, a desire for settlement and prolonged thinking and discussion. Further action is often necessary for psychological completeness and in order to expand and exemplify ideas sufficiently to make a real settlement. William James pointed out that it is psychologically unhealthy to feel an emotion or impulse and not give it fairly prompt expression in action. In certain situations and with certain people action must be immediate—action which makes for a new order and thereby resists the old order.[1]

Richard Gregg points to the need for nonviolent peacemaking to sometimes be action oriented. The nonviolent peacemaker cannot always avoid conflict due to her belief system, and sometimes she must even initiate the conflict in order to help rectify an oppressive situation.

Gregg's concern for finding an outlet for emotional energy was affirmed by a conflict theorist, Paul Keller, in an interview.

> One cannot continually suppress his anger and remain healthy. There are a number of case histories that are dramatic because they are pictures of people who are nice guys, who always did what they were supposed to do, and then who one day committed tremendously violent acts, in an apparently unprovoked environment.

Albert Keim commented on the unhealthy tendency to repress emotions.

> . . . I'm impressed by the fact anger and its manifestations are necessary and healthy, and passivity as it's so often understood in terms of pacifism is very unhealthy. . . . There is a very interesting study of a black psychologist who studied . . . [a] program in Mississippi . . . [where] hundreds of white and black college students [were sent] to register blacks in the delta. . . . One of the things that struck him was . . . the enormous amount of physical battering these people took. Every day they were . . . harrassed and often beaten . . . and jailed and they turned the other cheek . . . because they were nonviolent. But he was impressed by the fact that when he visited their unit houses, the place was in shambles. The furniture was busted up, the windows were knocked out. And the kids themselves spent most of their time beating up on each other. And his point was that . . . they beat up on each other . . . [in order to vent their anger because] they couldn't against the police and the white folk.

As the nonviolent peacemaker enters conflict he needs to find ways to release his emotional energy. Gregg contends that nonviolent peacemaking helps to solve the problem of how to redirect emotional energy in a positive manner once the conflict situation begins. Gregg's affirmation of a nonviolent outlet for emotional energy was supported by Martin Luther King, Jr.

> 'The nonviolent approach provides an answer to the long debated question of gradualism *versus* immediacy. On the one hand it prevents one from falling into the sort of patience which is an excuse for donothingism and escapism, ending up in standstillism. On the other hand, it saves one from irresponsible words which estrange without reconciling and the hasty judgment which is blind to the necessities of the social process. It recognizes the need for moving toward the goal of justice with wise restraint and calm reasonableness. But it also recognizes the immorality of slowing up in the move toward justice and capitulating to the guardians of an unjust status

quo. It recognizes that social change cannot come overnight. But it causes one to work as if it were a possibility the next morning.'[2]

Rather than using one's energy to respond violently, the nonviolent peacemaker redirects human energy and anger through the channel of nonviolent action, in order to promote justice constructively.

Turning Potential Violence into Nonviolent Resistence

Most of the representatives of the historic peace churches considered conflict as inevitable and found nonviolent peacemaking in protest as the only viable option for the human species, if annihilation is to be avoided. They did not guarantee the effectiveness of nonviolent peacemaking, but found it to be the most constructive option for dealing with conflict. One person felt that nonviolent peacemaking is a good alternative to violent defense, but he could not guarantee, as some people do, that it will always work. Another individual stated that Gene Sharp has emphasized the long-range and sometimes even the short-range effectiveness of a nonviolent peacemaking stance. This demonstrates that more than faith can support the nonviolent peacemaking position; it can sometimes be effective. A number of peacemakers see time as running out for the human race unless violent activity ceases. Their hope is that people will recognize that nonviolent peacemaking can be a constructive alternative to violence or avoidance of conflict. Nonviolent peacemaking works to resolve a conflict situation in a constructive fashion. One person relayed a message that Kenneth Boulding has stated: Humanity may be pushed to find nonviolent peacemaking as the only live option for dealing with conflict in the future, due to our ability or capacity to annihilate ourselves. Paul Keller summarizes the feeling expressed by a number of the representatives of the historic peace churches.

I see violent options as dead-end options for us. I think it is entirely possible that we will not long have a chance to search for more alternatives simply because we have not yet been willing to give up what we think are viable [violent] options. James Michener has helped me think about this by pointing out in *Centennial* that the dinosaur existed for 150 million years, and man's existence is probably very brief, maybe only 2 million years. . . . We have gotten the impression that it's [man's class of life] a forever thing. I don't think that is at all a viable position. So when I look at violence in the world, it seems to me that if man has within him the resources to save his own class of life, then he has to look at something other than violent options.

This inquiry points emphatically to the need for nonviolent approaches to conflict; nonviolent peacemaking in protest may be a needed constructive way of redirecting human energy. As Atlee Beechy stated, nonviolent peacemaking is a form of constructive communication. Nonviolent peacemaking attempts to approach change in a manner that affirms the sanctity of all human life, yet works for the goal of human justice and peace.

When nonviolent peacemaking is used to protest an oppressive situation, concern for both oppressor and oppressed is present. Nonviolent peacemaking cannot be equated with a tactic. Leroy Pelton in *The Psychology of Nonviolence* clarifies the difference between a tactic and a nonviolent peacemaking protest of resistance that is grounded in concern for both oppressed and oppressor. Pelton states that the street protests in Chicago during the 1968 Democratic Convention were not examples of nonviolent peacemaking.

> Provocation of the police through throwing things at them or taunting them by calling them 'pigs' and directing other verbal insults at them is not consistent with the nonviolent philosophy, which entails treating the adversary with dignity and respect. Calling the police pigs is destructive behavior in that it increases polarization and mitigates against reconciliation. Nonviolent action ideally strives to be constructive and reconciliatory. Not all protest demonstrations in which the demonstrators do not initiate or even react with violence are necessarily nonviolent.[3]

Pelton reveals that there is a distinction between nonviolent peacemaking in protest as a tactic or technique and nonviolent peacemaking in protest carried on in the spirit of reconciliation of both parties in conflict.

This distinction between nonviolent peacemaking as a tactic and nonviolent peacemaking grounded in an attitude of concern for both parties in conflict is a distinction that may not be recognized by all nonviolent peacemakers. Some nonviolent peacemakers tend to reject the use of nonviolent peacemaking in protest and resistance altogether because of their reluctance to use coercion and power. One peacemaker stated:

> . . . nonviolence, it seems to me, is a particular technique for what I'll call . . . a certain kind of coercion, it's coercion without arms. But it's nevertheless coercion. I have a strong reaction against nonviolence, because it seems to me it's merely coercion without a shotgun.

The concern to not use coercive techniques is supported by the fact that power is often viewed as incongruent with the goals of nonviolent peacemaking. The use of power may be questioned to such an extent as to paralyze the ability of the peacemaker to protest at all. One individual stated:

> In our tradition, we've always said we turn the other cheek. . . . I don't buy that at all. . . . there are levels of power I would be willing to embrace. . . . the degree [of power] has to do with the question of life.

There is both an aversion to the use of power, in that one would prefer to turn the other cheek and avoid the conflict situation, and an awareness that power can be used constructively in order to save a human life. Power that seeks to destroy the opponent is not a level of power advocated in nonviolent peacemaking. Power used to confront an opponent that is grounded in concern for both parties in the conflict situation can be a compatible component in nonviolent peacemaking.

Joan Bondurant in an article, "Force, Violence and the Innocent Dilemma," illuminates why power utilization is sometimes an uncomfortable situation for a nonviolent peacemaker. Bondurant contends that conflict is a never ending part of human life. She is concerned with eliminating violent conflict and wielding a nonviolent force of persuasion, resistance, and restraint. Thus, she differentiates between force and violence. Her conception of force is rooted in nonviolent peacemaking.

> The longing for surcease from all conflict is a longing for the end of time. Man's objective cannot be that of the elimination of conflict, but the discovery of means for conducting conflict creatively. . . . But the exploration of force without violence has only begun.[4]

Bondurant considers force rooted in nonviolence a positive alternative to violence. Bondurant is pointing to a constructive use of power that can be used in a nonviolent show of force of resistance.

A number of the representatives of the historic peace churches commented on the writings of Gene Sharp. He has attempted to show how power can be used in a constructive manner in nonviolent protest and defense. At Manchester College, Gene Sharp addressed an assembly that included a number of the interviewees composing the text of this inquiry. One individual related that what he appreciated about Gene Sharp was that he is not naively idealistic. He had confronted a tough problem with a tough answer. Neil Katz, Director of the Program of Nonviolent Conflict and Change at Syracuse University, stated a similar concern. He said that the work of Sharp, Bondurant and Pelton have provided new insights for " . . . the people who want to struggle openly . . . [they] are resisting now and are beginning to find out how to wield power and use power . . . through nonviolent action." Power need not be a destructive happening; it can be utilized in nonviolent protest and defense in the hope of maintaining or establishing a peaceful and just existence.

Gandhi visualized the need to use power in order to overcome the oppressive situation that India was experiencing. Gandhi's aim was to resist evil, but not with evil means. He felt that ahimsa was the only way to know truth, in that it was an approach to evil through love, noninjury, and nonviolence. Gandhi embraced nonviolent means whenever he entered a power struggle that required him to confront what he perceived as wrong. Gandhi felt that power utilized in the form of nonviolent resistance was sometimes necessary to emphasize neglected concerns of the oppressed peoples. Horace Alexander provides some insight into Gandhi's view of power and resistance.

> Long ago, in my early association with him I asked Gandhi how it was that patient, persuasive, generous to his opponents as I saw him to be, he would seem to abandon all this, and resort to direct action [nonviolent resistance]. . . . The essence of his answer was this. People are often so deeply rooted in ancient prejudices, which they assume to be unshakable truth, that they can never be touched by reason alone. Shock treatment alone may lead them to examine their presuppositions, so that they may begin to see that they must revise their fundamental beliefs.[5]

Power utilized in the form of protest based in nonviolent peacemaking can open up issues that the persons in power tend to be unaware of or ignore. Once the issue is brought to attention, a seeming increase in conflict may occur, when actually the conflict has only been made present rather than suppressed.

Theodore Roszak provided illuminating material on the problem of power, as he wrote an imaginary dialogue between Gandhi and Churchill, in a short article entitled, "Gandhi and Churchill: A Dialogue on Power." In this fictitious exchange, Churchill refuses to refer to Gandhi as a statesman. He can acknowledge that people followed him as children followed Stephen of Vendome on the Children's Crusade. But, being a Pied Piper does not mean that an individual has the status of a statesman. A statesman has a realistic appreciation of power and pursues timely and appropriate goals. Churchill goes on to say that Gandhi played on the populace's religious sensitivities and stirred their moral passions to gain their support. Gandhi countered this accusation by stating that Churchill had accomplished the same goal, of inciting the moral passions of his countrymen, in order to win the war effort, through his eloquent BBC broadcasts.

Although both attempted to arouse the moral passion of the people in Roszak's imaginary dialogue, Churchill sees a distinction between the approaches of the two leaders. Churchill asserts that his appreciation of power includes the necessity of compromise, while Gandhi stubbornly clings to his hopeless idealism. Idealism at the people's expense can promote needless suffering and death. Gandhi's response is that Churchill's concept of power allows the means to be justified by the end. Gandhi rejects Churchill's assertion that:

> The weapons change, but not the ancient principle: *si vis pacem, para bellum.* In 1953 I said, 'When the advance to destructive weapons enables everyone to kill everyone else, nobody will want to kill anyone at all.' This is what deterrence amounts to, and what it requires is that we arm and remain armed as never before in history.[6]

Gandhi refuses to accept Churchill's understanding of power. Gandhi relates:

> Ours is the age of the masses and of massive violence, a revolutionary age that requires a revolution in our conception of power. And this, for all my failures and miscalculations, is what I offered as a pioneer of nonviolence: a revolution in the meaning of power which called for 'the vindication of truth by the infliction of suffering not on the opponent but on one's self.'[7]

Roszak's imaginary dialogue emphasizes the need for power, which seeks compatibility of means and ends and works not to dominate the oppressor, but to free both parties in the conflict.

Power is a part of every relationship that is structured in Camus' words as "executioner and victim." To deal with the oppressor and oppressed relationship, the victim must utilize power. Power can be used in a violent fashion to overthrow the person in power, or in a manner congruent with Gandhi's concern for means and ends. Power used in nonviolent peacemaking resistance or protest works for a change that will aid the oppressed without destroying the oppressor. This dual response is an action that can free the humanity of both executioner and victim.

Power and Love in Nonviolent Resistance

The Jewish philosopher, Martin Buber, has articulated his concern for seeing power and love as compatible, essential companions. The following poem states Buber's concern quite clearly.

Power and Love

Our hope is too new and too old —
I do not know what would remain to us
We love not transfigured power
And power not straying love.

Do not protest: 'Let love alone rule!'
Can you prove it true?
But resolve: Every morning
I shall concern myself anew about the boundary
Between the love-deed — Yes and the power-deed — No
And pressing forward honor reality.

We cannot avoid
Using power,
Cannot escape the compulsion
To afflict the world
So let us, cautious in diction
And mighty in contradiction,
Love powerfully.[8]

Power can be used in the act of resisting another in a fashion compatible with nonviolent peacemaking. The oppressed can stand her own ground while working to change the oppressive situation in the spirit of love. Power guided by love aids the oppressed in foregoing the temptation of striving for revenge motivated by hate.

Martin Luther King, Jr. also affirms the possible congruence of power and love. King states:

There is nothing wrong with power if power is used correctly. . . .
What is needed is a realization that power without love is reckless
and abusive and love without power is sentimental and anaemic.
Power at its best is love implementing the demands of justice, and
justice at its best is power correcting everything that stands against
love.[9]

Often an individual may need to stand up for herself and assert her own power. To allow the other to always have his own way even when his actions appear wrong is love without strength of conviction and the power to oppose wrong. But a power that attempts to manipulate the other for personal gain without concern and care for that person's welfare is a destructive weapon that ignores the humanity of the other.

In nonviolent peacemaking the individual can test the compatibility or noncompatibility of power and love by applying a test pointed to by Gandhi. Gandhi saw two types of nonviolence: "nonviolence of the weak" and "nonviolence of the strong." A nonviolent peacemaker who uses nonviolence merely because the means for a violent response are not available is engaged in a tactic of power. He is utilizing a "nonviolence of the weak." An individual who pursues a nonviolent peacemaking resistance or protest even when violent options are available affirms a "nonviolence of the strong."[10] Power is accepted as necessary to change the situation; but this power is enveloped in love, in that there is concern for both oppressor and oppressed. Taking the life of the other is rejected as an option.

The combination of power and love in the form of nonviolent peacemaking in protest and resistance can be a form of constructive communication that can reveal an alternative to current values or beliefs of those in power. Sometimes a person must offer a nonviolent protest or resistance as a form of constructive communication that stands up against prevailing opinion. A. J. Muste, the Executive Secretary of the Fellowship of Reconciliation between 1942 and 1955, attempted to emphasize the need for constructively protesting the mistaken ideals of government structures when they are at odds with the goals of a peaceful and just society. In his essay, *Of Holy Disobedience,* he states that docility and lack of responsibility, not cruelty will be the destruction of the human. He recounts an introductory chapter by Kay Boyle to a volume of short stories about Germany during the Nazi regime, *The Smoking Mountain.* Muste attempts to emphasize the need for action in the form of nonviolent protest and resistance.

> She [Kay Boyle] tells about a woman, professor of philology in a Hessian university who said of the German experience with Nazism: 'It was a gradual process.' When the first *Jews Not Wanted* signs went up, 'there was never any protest against them, and, after a few months, not only we, but even the Jews who lived in that town, walked past without noticing any more that they were there. Does it seem impossible to you that this should have happened to civilized people anywhere?'
>
> The philology professor went on to say that after a while she put up a picture of Hitler in her classroom. After twice refusing to take the oath of allegiance to Hitler, she was persuaded by her students to take it. 'They argued that in taking this oath, which so many anti-Nazis had taken before me, *I was committing myself to nothing . . .* '[11]

Muste then states that a decision by a nonviolent peacemaking group to openly protest the beginnings of Nazism might have awakened the country to the realization that they lived on the edge of holocaust.

A. J. Muste was influenced by a writer who saw the insanity of war during the 1800s, Henry David Thoreau. In an essay entitled *On the Duty of Civil Disobedience,* Thoreau states that an individual must be a human being first and only then a subject to some governmental process. The human needs to cultivate an appreciation for the right, whether or not it includes the law. A century before the second World War, Thoreau stated his concern that a human must at times protest and resist; Thoreau's writing reveals that the reluctance to challenge another is not a new phenomenon.

> There are thousands who are *in opinion* opposed to slavery *and* to war, who yet in effect do nothing to put an end to them; who, esteeming themselves children of Washington and Franklin sit down with their hands in their pockets, and say that they do not know what to do, and do nothing . . .[12]

The point is clear that both Thoreau and Muste offer a vital message to those who affirm nonviolent peacemaking. To never challenge the governmental powers can implicitly support potentially unjust and immoral decisions.

Sometimes a nonviolent peacemaker needs to challenge rather than acquiesce to authority. To paraphrase one peacemaker, most people long for the good, but their understanding of authority often doesn't allow them to work for the good. Both Thoreau and Muste are offering a different understanding of authority; it needs to be questioned and challenged when it does not ensure a just and peaceful world for all people. To allow oppression to prosper is to become the silent accomplice to those oppressive actions. As long as an individual accepts the decisions of a despotic force, that force wields all the authority and power. It is only when one rejects the authority of that force that their power begins to weaken.

The nonviolent peacemaker may need to elicit conflict from others in order to bring attention to an oppressive situation. Power used in a nonviolent peacemaking protest and/or resistance challenges the oppressor in order to affirm the ideals of peace and justice for all peoples. But the challenge is a nonviolent peacemaking protest which allows the other to continue to live and make decisions. The protest does not seek to conquer. This form of protest is stated quite clearly by one individual: " . . . nonviolence has to do with refusing, with not allowing the other person's freedom to make a decision to be taken away. . . . it refuses to take away the other person's right to decide. If I kill that other person, obviously I've taken away the other person's right to decide . . . " Nonviolent peacemaking in protest and resistance challenges, but always provides the opponent with his freedom to live, which allows him to make decisions without fear of death. Power needs to be guided by a love that manifests concern for the humanity of both oppressor and oppressed. Power is sometimes necessary to make one's voice heard; however, power used in nonviolent peace-making should not be used to ignore or destroy the other.

Part Three

Peacemaking: The Radical Commitment

Chapter Seven

Commitment or Narcissism?

A number of the representatives of the historic peace churches viewed the human being as often motivated by selfish concerns. One person stated that he considered the human basically selfish. The particular expression of that selfishness may change from culture to culture, but the basic self-centered motivation seems to always be present. Another individual stated that self-centeredness seems to be a human quality; self rather than others and God are placed at the center of one's life: " . . . there is a fundamental flaw in man. And we call that sin, arrogance, or egotism." The problem becomes how does a person move from individual good to the good of the species? How does an individual get another who is well off to forego some of her benefits for others?

The magnitude of selfish concerns is pointed to by Allen Deeter, the Director of the Peace Studies Program at Manchester College. He said that if human beings become even more trained in self-interested viciousness, then destruction of humankind is a real possibility. The representatives of the historic peace churches did not foresee a positive and productive future for human beings if they continue to engage in self-concern to the exclusion of their fellows. The human seemingly has forgotten that he is a part of all existence. Some individuals are not content to be a part of life; they prefer to be the central point. Their own selves become the important consideration. They may involve themselves in activities with others, but only if they believe those activities will lead to their own fulfillment. They tend to use activities and others to fulfill themselves, rather than appreciating the importance of involvement in activities with others in order to broaden their own horizon of possibilities. One peacemaker summarized this concern regarding the human's self-centered orientation.

> I contend that most people do not grow beyond the place where they are willing to place their faith and commitment in nations or family. . . . People do not usually accept values which are higher than preservation. I find that the values taught by the great philosophies or the great religions of the world are the ones that go beyond that. They encourage love, justice, and truth.

Human Conceit

The seriousness of the human's tendency to be self-centered is affirmed in a work by Gregory Rochlin, *Man's Aggression: The Defense of the Self.* Rochlin contends that the human is narcissistic or self-centered, and when the human's self-esteem is threatened an aggressive response results. He says that as the human's narcissistic interest in herself increases, a corresponding interest in one's relation to others diminishes. Rochlin not only sees aggression as a possible response to lowered self-esteem, but he also identifies passivity as a narcissistic response that masks aggressive impulses. He considers passivity to be a psychological defense. A passive response is uniquely human in that there is no parallel reaction in animal existence. Thus, Rochlin sees narcissism as potentially destructive in two ways: (1) a person may respond aggressively to another, or (2) an individual may respond passively, which may do violence to himself.[1] Rochlin's analysis of narcissism is related to nonviolent peacemaking, but its value is limited by the importance he places on the concept of self-esteem. One's mode of being-in-the-world is more fundamental than self-esteem. If one accepts a being-in-the-world that places a primary emphasis on self-fulfillment, only then does injury to one's self-esteem begin to promote the responses Rochlin described.

If one does knowingly or unknowingly seek one's own self-fulfillment, then one may be inclined to use an aggressive response toward the other in order to protect his own self-esteem. This can be done in a physical response or a verbal confrontation. This desire to enhance one's own self-esteem may lead a person to enter a conflict situation for the wrong reasons. A person may want to ventilate anger against another to improve her own self-image. A confrontation may be used to embarrass or humiliate an opponent in order to reinforce the confronter's self-concept as the promoter of a morally superior cause. The issue of disagreement no longer is the primary concern; it becomes a vehicle that allows the confronter to enhance his own self-concept and thus fulfill the self.

Some nonviolent peacemakers, like many other humans, have knowingly and/or unknowingly accepted a being-in-the-world that embraces self-fulfillment. This leads some nonviolent peacemakers to affirm a being-in-the-world that fits the analysis pointed to by Rochlin. Concern for self-esteem and self-image become paramount considerations. A number of the representatives of the historic peace churches pointed to this problem; they stated that some nonviolent peacemakers are more concerned about their own self-images than the issue of peace: " . . . there's many a person who is opposed to war . . . who doesn't manifest that style of life in a lot of other respects." Another person stated that those who claim themselves nonviolent peacemakers have done a great injustice to the total life style by being so personally argumentative and abrasive.

An individual may seek to gain a feeling of worth and importance from her self-image as a defender of the oppressed. The issue of peace becomes a vehicle for the reinforcement of one's self-image. In the pursuit to reinforce one's self-image, the humanity of those who disagree with one's view of the world may be ignored. The desire to promote a peaceful world for both oppressed and oppressor is forgotten. As one peacemaker stated, nonviolent peacemaking can be a self-serving stance. During his seminary education, he became acquainted with the writings of Reinhold Niebuhr. At that time he became conscious of the possibility of a nonviolent peacemaking position being a self-serving life style. A nonviolent peacemaker who accepts the importance of self-fulfillment may use the goal of peace for his own development. His primary goal may no longer be a peaceful and just world for all people. He may become more concerned with enhancing his self-image as a voice for the oppressed than with working for the attainment of a peaceful and just human society.

One person pointed to why some nonviolent peacemakers might knowingly and/or unknowingly affirm the self-fulfillment mode of being-in-the-world. He contended that theologians and psychologists have tended to go their separate ways since World War II. Some sensitivity trainers attempt to get people in touch with their feelings and real selves without encouraging an examination of the presuppositions upon which this approach is based. They ignore the fact that each view of the human is inherently presuppositional. It seems that some humanists have failed to do their theological homework. Another person stated, " . . . humanism is fragile and needs under strenuous circumstances to be sustained by faith. I think the movement of the 60s among the youth was a demonstration of this. There was a great deal of moral activity, but it was rootless and so it withered away in a hurry." A nonviolent peacemaker needs to question the self-fulfillment assumption promoted by some humanists that an individual should only be responsible for his own feelings.

A self-fulfillment orientation to the world is not sanctioned and promoted by a number of authors involved in third force or humanistic psychology. The goal of third force psychology is laudable. An effort to recognize and support the worth of the person and personal freedom has characterized the movement. However, this orientation has tended to emphasize the importance of the person's immediate self too much. An individual's relation to tasks and others is not given sufficient emphasis. A person is encouraged to get in touch with her own horizon, rather than broadening herself by attending to her relation to tasks and others. This view of the person has permeated much of the intellectual and personal climate of those who affirm humanistic principles.

If a person accepts his own importance without recognition of the need to relate to tasks and others to discover new possibilities and opportunities, an inflated view of self may occur. This may lead an individual to attempt to express his "true" self or "inner" feelings when addressing another. But as the goal of expressing who one "actually is" becomes paramount, then the displaying of abrasive actions toward another becomes more acceptable. The 1960s and 1970s have been so concerned with allowing each individual's human potential to unfold, that others are sometimes forgotten. This hope of fulfilling one's own self often results in a self-centered orientation, in which a person feels little or no responsibility for others. An abrasive individual may be true to her "inner" self without regard for how the other may be hurt by her comments. An individual tends to ignore the other's hurt by accepting phrases such as, "I can only take responsibility for my own behavior; I can't take responsibility for another." This orientation is revealed quite dramatically in the Gestalt Prayer by Fritz Perls.

> I do my thing, and you do your thing.
> I am not in this world to live up to your expectations
> And you are not in this world to live up to mine.
> You are you, and I am I.
> And if by chance we find each other, it's beautiful.
> If not, it can't be helped.[2]

The Gestalt Prayer reveals an attitude in which oneself, not one's relation to others becomes the primary concern. This orientation may be reflected in a nonviolent peacemaker's address to another. An individual may become more concerned about his own self-fulfillment or his own self-image as a protector of the oppressed than his original goal of peace and justice. A nonviolent peacemaker who accepts this self-centered orientation, like any other person who affirms this posture, becomes primarily concerned with her own responsibility and does not take much responsibility for the other in everyday life. The peacemaker may talk about caring for all people in the abstract, but in daily living, he may not. He may feel responsibility to himself to announce to the world that it is wrong to kill and maim others, but he may care little for his opponents except to win them over to his particular philosophical view. This orientation to the other is pointed to quite clearly by one representative of the historic peace churches. He stated a concern that nonviolent peacemaking is sometimes:

> . . . tainted by a kind of middle class snobbishness, and self-righteousness . . . saying that we are enlightened, and those poor ignorant people out there in a state of darkness—if only we could do something about them. And it seems to me that that very attitude perverted the good . . . values and beliefs.

It is this self-righteousness that is revealed when the person expresses his own self without regard for his opponent's feelings or humanity. When the nonviolent peacemaker forgets the humanity of the other, she begins to affirm an orientation similar to Perl's Prayer. She takes responsibility only for announcing the cause, not for affirming the humanity of both oppressed and oppressor. The concern becomes the winning of the confrontation and the sustenance of her image as a nonviolent peacemaker, rather than relating herself to the task of peace because it is an important cause.

What Is Beyond Self-Interest?

The nonviolent peacemaker who accepts the need for compatibility of means and ends needs to care for both the oppressor and oppressed in the change process, not just affirm herself. Walter Tubbs recognized the limitation of attempting to find only self-fulfillment. He spoke of the need to confirm the other, as he responded to Perl's Gestalt Prayer.

> If I just do my thing and you do yours,
> We stand in danger of losing each other
> And ourselves.
>
> I am not in this world to live up to your expectations;
> But I am in this world to confirm you

As a unique human being,
And to be confirmed by you.

We are fully ourselves only in relation to each other;
The I detached from a Thou
Disintegrates.

I do not find you by chance;
I find you by an active life
Of reaching out.

Rather than passively letting things happen to me,
I can act intentionally to make them happen.

I must begin with myself, true;
But I must not end with myself:
The truth begins with two.[3]

Tubb's response to Perls points to the importance of recognizing that responsibility only to oneself is not sufficient for a full and productive existence.

A number of writers from the social sciences and the humanities affirm Tubbs' statement that truth begins with two. To only deal with oneself, rather than relate oneself to other people or other tasks, is to fail to fulfill one's potential. If a person is always reflecting on himself he will miss ongoing life experience. Maurice Friedman has stated his concern that self-realization or self-fulfillment is not the fullest orientation to the world, although many philosophers and psychologists propose self-oriented themes. Friedman states:

> The concept of self-realization lies at the heart of Sartre's 'project,' of Heidegger's realization of one's ownmost, not-to-be-outstripped, nonrelational possibility; of John Dewey's ethics of potentiality, and the thought of such varied psychologists and psychoanalysts as Rollo May, Carl Rogers, Medard Boss, Erich Fromm, Karen Horney, and Abraham Maslow. As a holistic approach to the person which sees his or her future actuality from the present possibility, it represents a decisive step forward toward the human image. Nevertheless this approach is not concrete or serious enough to grapple with the problem of finding authentic personal direction.[4]

The constructive contribution of the self-realization or self-fulfillment theme is that the importance of the self is recognized, but the downfall of this way of viewing the world is that the significance of the other is forgotten. Self-actualization cannot occur in a vacuous state without other humans. Significant others contribute to each human being's growth and development.

Brewster Smith in his article, "On Self-Actualization: A Trans-ambivalent Examination of a Focal Theme in Maslow's Psychology," affirms many of Friedman's comments. Smith contends that too much significance has been drawn from one informal study completed by Abraham Maslow. Maslow examined the personal characteristics of fifty-one contemporary and historical figures who he believed exemplified the ideal of psychological health. Maslow contended that self-actualizing individuals " . . . seem to be fulfilling themselves and to be doing the best that they are capable of doing, reminding us of Nietzsche's exhortation, 'Become what thou art!' "[5] Maslow's work gave support to numerous individuals in humanistic or third force psychology, who are proponents of self-development. Smith raises a significant concern regarding this approach. If the human rejects the notion that good will always emerge from another, then the development of each person's potentiality may not be for the common good.

> If an Unseen Hand is absent in human history, then self-actualization in the sense of growth process does not inevitably lead to the common good. 'Doing what comes naturally' is not enough. The emphasis in Maslow's writings is on the fulfillment of the individual, and the encounter movement that draws upon his writings has become much more flagrantly individualistic.[6]

Ironically, Brewster Smith has revealed that the humanistic movement, which often attempts to provide a counter-culture alternative to the prevailing survival of the fittest philosophy that permeates much of western culture, has accepted an individualistic and self-centered philosophical stance as the very foundation of its protest. Smith states that the followers of Maslow have out-self-actualized the father of the concept by emphasizing self-fulfillment too much. Maslow himself saw other humans and the importance of constructive achievements as integral to the personality of a self-actualizing person. "Not only do self-actualizing people tend to be altruists; but he [Maslow] notes that "the basic needs can be fulfilled only by and through other human beings."[7] Thus, in the western intellectual climate, it is not surprising that an individual would fall prey to the ethic of self-realization or self-fulfillment. In the words of David Eller: "Freedom of the late 1960s that was caught up in the phrase 'doing your own thing,' is a negative concept. There needs to be an interpersonal or social good that one finds his meaning in." Caring only for oneself in order to actualize one's potentials is not a constructive alternative. The nonviolent peacemaker needs to resist the temptation of seeking self-realization over the importance of human peace and justice.

Maurice Friedman summarizes the criticism of attempting to fulfill one's own potential. He states that the human cannot " . . . ignore the possibility of a tragic conflict between realizing one's potentialities to the full and playing one's part in an historical situation which may call on one to sacrifice this realization [of self], and perhaps life itself."[8] The nonviolent peacemaker indeed may have to give up her potential or even her life in working for human justice. If an individual's primary mission becomes self-fulfillment, the world in which he lives is likely to be forgotten. Exploitation, hunger, injustice, and violence permeate throughout the world, and individuals must share in the responsibility to correct these problems. One individual said:

> My hope is that mankind will use the intelligence with which he has evolved to invent and operate social (international) machinery (institutions) with which he can resolve conflicts without resort to force, and which will eliminate exploitation of man by man, and result in a just social order.

Desmond Bittinger stated that the human must work toward an international government and an international understanding that all the earth's resources are to be shared, not hoarded. Another peacemaker put the concern quite succinctly. His hope was that people would begin to take the commandment to "Love one another," seriously. The dreams and goals that the representatives of the historic peace churches announced will not come into being if the sole concern is to fulfill one's own potential. To promote a world of peace and justice requires a nonviolent peacemaker to pursue that goal, not the aspiration of merely fulfilling her own self.

If a nonviolent peacemaker affirms the need to care for both oppressor and oppressed, self-fulfillment may be incompatible with peace-oriented goals, such as those described by representatives of the historic peace churches. As Friedman mentioned earlier, the historical situation may call the person to do what he perceives is right even though that action may be contrary to self-fulfillment. Thus, for Friedman the aim of self-fulfillment has some major limitations, which he feels are not inherent in the being-in-the-world of the paradox of self-fulfillment. A person who accepts the paradox of self-fulfillment does not see her own development or growth as the aim or goal; rather it is a by-product of one's aim or commitment. Friedman contends that the more a person attempts to fulfill himself the less likely he will succeed in the endeavor. The notion of the paradox of self-fulfillment points to the importance of the human never becoming a goal or end product if she is to continually become herself. An individual does not fulfill himself in a vacuum. Life is a doing activity of meeting people, ideas and events. The human must refocus attention from herself to a relation to a task or another in order to enrich her being. If a person attempts only to fulfill himself, he will miss the ongoing activities about him that may actually allow fulfillment to occur. Friedman contends that:

> . . . those psychologists who seek to derive a direction-giving image of the human from the concept of self-realization . . . must recognize that self-realization cannot be made *the goal* either of therapy or of life, however indispensible it is as a by-product and corollary of a true life. . . . For this is the age-old paradox! We are called upon to realize ourselves, yet to aim directly at so doing is self-defeating. You *begin* with yourself, but you do not *aim* at yourself . . . [9]

Friedman contends that if a human commits herself to what seems worthy of action, then self-fulfillment may potentially occur as a by-product of her commitment.

Viktor Frankl also stresses the theme that self-fulfillment or happiness for oneself is not a goal, but rather a happenstance of a committed life. Frankl was able to develop a method of therapy which he called logotherapy. The basis for his understanding of the human person is meaning—can the human discover a meaning for his own existence? He does not refer to the happiness that is supposed to accompany the full development of a person's potential. His concern is that an individual discover something beyond herself that is worthy of engagement. Frankl considers the pleasure principle self-defeating. The more an individual attempts to fulfill his potential, the more likely he is to fail. Caring only for oneself is like the action of a boomerang. As people work only for their own needs, they are always missing the target and ending up with their attention or boomerang on themselves again. Only by committing oneself to a task or another is there a chance that one will fulfill one's potentialities. [10]

Frankl contends that his mode of therapy is helpful to the human in search of meaning and commitment to values greater than herself. He states that he attempts to teach his patients reverence for life, a phrase often articulated by Albert Schweitzer. But in order for an individual to have reverence for life, he must have a task to which he can commit himself. Frankl feels that his task is to help individuals dedicate their lives to values which may indirectly lead to fulfillment of self. He proposes a kind of Copernican Revolution regarding the question of the fulfilled life. Life asks questions of the human, who must respond by fulfilling life tasks, not directly seeking self-fulfillment.[11] Frankl's thesis is that the neuroses of meaninglessness permeate the western world. Self-fulfillment is an attempt to fill that vacuum, but instead it is contributing to it.

Maurice Friedman's and Viktor Frankl's announcement of the paradox of self-fulfillment provides a significant alternative to a self-fulfillment orientation to the world. But there needs to be an even more radical break from the concept of self-fulfillment. The paradox of self-fulfillment tends to emphasize a cause-effect relationship, no matter how tentative, between commitment to a task and self-fulfillment as a by-product. The paradox of self-fulfillment leaves the person hoping for self-fulfillment as an indirect result or by-product of commitment. The paradox of self-fulfillment is an improvement of means in that a person needs to commit herself to something other than the direct pursuit of self-fulfillment. But the goal of self-fulfillment remains the same; only it is viewed as a by-product, rather than as an aim.[12] Both self-fulfillment and the paradox of self-fulfillment are directly or indirectly oriented toward fulfilling oneself. Perhaps the peacemaker needs to embrace a radical commitment that breaks free of the goal of self-fulfilment, and works for peace because he feels it is right, not because some direct or indirect reward may be the result.

Such a proposal is not a moralistic ignoring of self; rather, the hope is to point to the importance of the nonviolent peacemaker being accessible to what is happening in the ongoing world. Accessibility implies that the nonviolent peacemaker attempts to be as open and aware of what is being announced in the ongoing happenings of the world as is possible in his own historical situation of the moment. The nonviolent peacemaker's accessibility to ongoing events is limited by the quest for self-fulfillment. Her focus of attention becomes the aim of self-fulfillment or the by-product of commitment to peace. If a person is concerned with the problem of self-fulfillment as an aim or as a by-product, he is likely to look for opportunities to fulfill himself or reflect on whether he was indirectly fulfilled by past activities, rather than attending to the ongoing problems of the moment. Preoccupation with direct or indirect self-fulfillment limits what one can see and understand. Ongoing activities and events may go unnoticed as one's focus of attention remains on her own horizon. Thus, the radical commitment accepts the philosophical notion of accessibility. Only by giving up the quest for self-fulfillment can one open oneself to the ongoing happenings in the world.

Accessibility to ongoing happenings in the world, which is a central notion in the radical commitment, is pointed to by Martin Buber. In "Elements of the Interhuman" Martin Buber differentiates between "being" and "seeming." He states that a person is "being" when he listens openly to the situation and relationship and then responds authentically to the address of the moment. An individual is "seeming" when she attempts to be something she is not in the situation and relationship.

> His look [being] is 'spontaneous,' 'without reserve'; of course he is not uninfluenced by the desire to make himself understood by the other, but he is uninfluenced by any thought of the idea of himself which he can or should awaken in the person whom he is looking at. His opposite [seeming] is different. Since he is concerned with the image which his appearance, and especially his look or glance, produces in the other, he 'makes' this look. With the help of the capacity, in greater or lesser degree peculiar to man, to make a definite element of his being appear in his look . . . [13]

Buber's concept of "seeming" reveals that a person can become so concerned about creating an image of himself that he will miss what is actually happening in the world. A person cannot listen and respond authentically to what is happening in the world when his focus of attention is consumed by attempting to portray a particular image of himself. The problem of self-fulfillment is a similar one. If a person is always looking for direct or indirect self-fulfillment, she will miss the ongoing happenings in the world. Both Buber's understanding of "being" and the notion of accessibility point to the importance of listening and responding to the living moment in an authentic fashion. Buber cautions against a preoccupation with image and self-fulfillment. For the nonviolent peacemaker, the radical commitment is an attempt to be sensitive to Buber's caution and listen to the ongoing events of the world and to respond as authentically as possible within the framework of nonviolent peacemaking.

Accessibility requires a person to be open to the events of the world and to respond to the address she hears with her whole being. Concern with direct and/or indirect self-fulfillment focuses one's attention on oneself, which allows the happenings in the world to go unheard and unattended. A nonviolent peacemaker cannot hear the cry of the world for justice, equality and human care if he is focused on self-fulfillment. The notion of accessibility in the radical commitment requires one to have the courage to listen to the address of ongoing happenings in the world, and then lend her personally unique response to the needs of the situation.

> We need the courage to address and the courage to respond. I use these terms in conscious contrast to Tillich's 'courage to be'; for we are not directly concerned with our being, and we cannot aim at it, or even at being a 'centered self,' in Tillich's phrase. The real courage that is asked of us — a greater and more terrifying courage — is the courage to respond, the courage to go out to meet the reality given in this moment, whatever its form. My trust is not that this reality will be such as I might wish it to be, but only that here and here only is meaning accessible to me . . . [14]

The nonviolent peacemaker's quest is the establishment of peace and justice in human relationships. This task can most fully be approached when one is accessible and open to ongoing events. Concern with direct or indirect self-fulfillment focuses one's attention on oneself; thus happenings in life that need correcting or would be beneficial to be aware of may go unnoticed because of one's self-concern. Working for peace from the stance of a radical commitment fosters an openness to the task of peace, not direct or indirect self-fulfillment. Accessibility to the ongoing happenings in the world will hopefully more fully allow the nonviolent peacemaker to use all her resources in attempting to complete a needed and awesome task of promoting a peaceful world.

Chapter Eight

From Independence to Interdependence

The need to move beyond a narrow nationalistic understanding of the world was pointed to by a number of the representatives of the historic peace churches. One individual who has traveled throughout the world as an anthropologist and nonviolent peacemaker said that as he talked with people in all parts of the globe, he found one intellectual commonplace on which both parties could agree. There is no hope for the world unless humanity learns to resolve its differences nonviolently. The earth is not the property of Christians or Buddhists, Capitalists or Communists; it belongs to all people. A nonviolent peacemaker must refuse to follow his government to war and actively help his international brothers and sisters by working to provide more equitable distribution of such necessities as food and water. One individual stated that he felt the human race was at a critical point in its history. Hopefully, in the future, an approximation of a global community will arise that will increase the human's chance of survival. Emmert Bittinger, in a recent conversation with the author, underscored this concern for world community:

> . . . to be human means to interact with other people in such a way that their well being is enhanced, appreciated and respected . . . which means that in international relations, one nation should not act purely on a selfish basis . . . we should see the world as a community, rather than just our nation as a community. . . . the sur-

vival of the world in the future is going to be based on common actions which enhance the humanity of all men, instead of just Americans.

Clearly, the above statements are pointing to a view of the world where the difficulty of one people becomes the anguish and task of all.

Global Community

The nonviolent peacemaker who affirms a global community is concerned with oppression and abuse of people throughout the world. Martin Luther King, Jr. manifested such a vision. During his struggle for his own people, he recognized the tyranny of a foreign force in Vietnam. Although King had to husband his energies for the cause of civil rights, he did not remain silent on global oppression. At a gathering in the Riverside Church in New York City, Dr. King delivered an address entitled, "Vietnam and the Struggle for Human Rights." This was not to be his last speech on the topic of Vietnam. Even as he received criticism from within the civil rights movement for his comments on Vietnam, he did not lessen his attack on the Vietnam tragedy. The following words catch the spirit of Martin Luther King, Jr.'s concern:

> Somehow this madness must cease. We must stop now. I speak as a child of God and brother to the suffering poor of Vietnam. I speak for those whose land is being laid waste, whose homes are being destroyed, whose culture is being subverted. I speak for the poor of America who are paying the double price of smashed hopes at home and death and corruption in Vietnam. I speak as a citizen of the world, for the world as it stands aghast at the path we have taken. I speak as an American to the leaders of my own nation. The great initiative in this war is ours. The initiative to stop it must be ours . . . [1]

Martin Luther King, Jr. saw the world as a community in which no human should be exploited or oppressed. He felt the United States should cease supporting corrupt governments and encourage nonviolent revolution by promoting an atmosphere throughout the world that affirmed disagreement and nonviolent struggle. He felt that the words of former President Kennedy would forever seem hypocritical unless the United States changed its suppressive tactics. Vietnam and other oppressive actions in the United States cause " . . . the words of the late John F. Kennedy [to] come back to haunt us . . . he said, 'Those who make peaceful revolution impossible will make violent revolution inevitable.' "[2] King saw global oppression and felt that only a concern for all people could encourage changes that were necessary for the dignity of the human people to be restored.

The nonviolent Quaker activist, George Lakey, has also emphasized the need to develop a global community. In his work, *Strategy for a Living Revolution,* he states that there must emerge a loyalty to the human race that transcends class and nationality. People need to see themselves as wrapped up in the concerns and needs of all humanity. Lakey says that the brotherhood of men and women is an idea that reaches back to the beginning of time. But now there is potential to actually feel akin to the other person's concerns. Social and economic forces are beginning to create an understanding of the other's life situations. For example, the mass media brought the suffering of the Vietnamese people right into the American living room. Lakey, who has devoted his life to seeking a world consciousness that will support nonviolent revolution throughout the world, states, "I have hoped that the sense of self which is rooted in community will be based primarily on the community of humankind . . . "[3] Lakey and the organization he works with, Movement for a New Society, are attempting to promote a world consciousness that they deem necessary to nonviolently protest and change inhumanity and injustice throughout the global community.

Possibly Lakey and King are pointing to an understanding of world community that is analogous to Albert Schweitzer's commitment to his medical profession.

> The Fellowship of those who bear the Mark of Pain. Who are the members of this fellowship? Those who have learned by experience what physical pain and bodily anguish mean, belong together all the world over; they are united by a secret bond.[4]

The bond that can potentially hold the world together is concern for the anguish and pain that typifies the global community. One person stated, "I think the real issue for pacifists right now is not so much war . . . but it has much more to do with the moral question of how one lives in the prosperous part of the world at a time when the rest of the world is suffering enormous disability." Another peacemaker stated that he wanted to affirm life as good, but he realized that for half the globe, life is utter hell. Half the people of the world languish in poverty. One fourth suffer from malnutrition and are near starvation. As he thought of the global community, he remembered a statement: "If you are not in pain, you are not paying attention to the world." Oppression and exploitation at both national and international levels are realities that construct the world. The commitment to work to change them may indeed lead one to work for a global community. One individual stated that as an anthropologist and traveler, he had the opportunity to talk with Albert Schweitzer, Dr. and Mrs. Leakey, and Arnold Toynbee. But the most impressive conversations occurred with so-called "primitive" people during archaeological digs. They talked about all of life as connected and related. The living process needs a variety of phenomena to work together. Global consciousness requires that same orientation; a great variety of people need to learn to work together in an harmonious fashion.

The representatives of the historic peace churches contended that as world resources become increasingly scarce, a feeling of interdependence may occur that could propel people to work for a global community.

> . . . I do think that people need to find universal values. They need to somehow be in touch with what it is that makes it possible to live a life that allows them to be a part of a community, a worldwide community. . . . I think the foundation stone on which that rests for me, is interdependence of life. I have a basic conviction that human beings cannot exist in any solitary fashion, and that any view that leads us to think of the individual as . . . the self-made man, or leads us to think that people can get along without each other, is a false view. So that I think that we start from the social fact of life, rather than from any individual fact. . . . Our very interdependence means that we must learn not to treat each other in exploitive or violent ways.

Another individual stated that he had taken youth to a seminar in Washington, D. C. He felt the title of that experience, "From Independence to Interdependence," described a needed transition in people's understanding of the world. The increasing scarcity of goods and resources may necessitate an increased interdependence of nations. This reality will either lead to even more competition between countries, or in the words of Paul Keller, lead to a recognition of world community.

> My hope lies in the recognition that we do stand on the edge of the abyss and that unless we can learn to live as a world community, we are not likely to live as nations. We are becoming more and more aware of our interdependence. We know now that we can help feed each other, and we're going to have to help feed each other or there will be massive violence. I guess my hope does lie in the potential crises.

The interdependence of people is an increasingly present reality. The human does, and will even more in the future, depend on his fellows if all are to survive.

Thomas Merton stressed the concept of interdependence in a profound and clear fashion in a short article that was the preface to the Vietnamese translation of "No Man Is an Island." Merton said that at the funeral of any human, the bell does, indeed, "toll for thee." For each individual being will meet the same fate of death. Merton contends that in this modern world, the death of a human being is not understood compassionately. Death is merely made more efficient and easier to inflict upon another. The human attempts to protect himself against death by imposing that state upon his opponent. Merton suggests that compassion is necessary to understand death and the true nature of life.

> Compassion teaches me that when my brother dies, I too die. Compassion teaches me that my brother and I are one. That if I love my brother, then my love benefits my own life as well, and if I hate my brother and seek to destroy him, I destroy myself as well.[5]

Merton states that a purely meditative life that is focused on individualism is "unreal," because the reality that "no man is an island" is either forgotten or ignored. Violence is based in the assumption of difference. "I am good, but the opponent is corrupt and evil; therefore I can legitimize saving myself and disposing of my enemy." Compassion and love recognize similarity in self and the opponent. Each has the hope of survival. The enemy is not the opponent; the enemy is war. Finally, Merton contended that a selfish life will never be fruitful; it contradicts the very nature of the human. When the human lives only for herself she becomes an "island" — an island of fear, suspicion, and hate. All her judgments and views of the world are governed by this untruth. The human being needs to recover her true vision, which allows her to see that each man and woman is a brother and sister — for "no man is an island."[6]

An interesting perspective on the problem of interdependence is often utilized in social scientific research. If a social scientist desires to be "practical," a happening or event is isolated and studied as an independent phenomenon. This method of analysis is not uncommon in the study of human interaction. Individuals attempt to be "practical" and study an event independently when in actuality a much larger interdependent system may need to be explored. A wife may be encouraged by her family to seek counseling. They may determine that she is the sole problem in the family. Yet the entire family system promotes the difficulty, not just one individual. Often the act of practicality, taking something out of its interrelated context and studying it independently, is an error if one wants to understand the original happening. An event or happening is defined by its context. To change its context is to change the phenomenon under investigation.

The vision for seeing ongoing happenings of the human as isolated and independent becomes, in Merton's terms, unreal. Individuals sometimes ignore the context from which the human comes, an interconnected social context. One person stated: " . . . I think to be human you have to be interactive with other people. . . . I don't think you can be human by yourself." Perhaps "practicality" is not isolating humans and human problems into unrelated independent categories. Possibly a vision of the interdependent nature of the human is a needed practicality, if the human is to survive. As Merton stated, an understanding of humans as individual isolated beings can legitimize the killing of something foreign to oneself. But the acceptance of interdependence of persons can promote an understanding that to love the other benefits oneself and to seek to destroy an opponent is to destroy part of oneself as well.

Viewing the world as an interdependent or an interrelated phenomenon is recognized as essential by Gregory Bateson. He rejected the notion of excessive individualism. Bateson believed that the human was arrogant and absurd when he attempted to convince himself that he was the "master of his fate" or the "captain of his soul." The environment, gestalt, or surrounding world needs to be taken into account if one is to understand a phenomenon. For Bateson, all of life is interdependent in that it is always *contextual*. The human is always surrounded by other life that affects her existence.[7]

One of the clearest indications of Bateson's viewing of life as interconnected or interdependent, is his understanding of schismogenesis. Schismogenesis is a relationship that has gotten out of control and is increasingly escalating. Bateson recognizes two types of schismogenic relationships that have snowballed beyond control. The first is a symmetrical schismogenic relationship, in which competition between equals has increased to a point of potential danger. For example, when the United States builds a new weapon, the Russians then build a more sophisticated armament, as has been the case in recent years. Symmetrical schismogenesis also helps explain the escalating nature of violence. As a person reacts to a physical attack, she may attempt to increase the violent conflict by confronting her opponent with even greater danger. The second type of schismogenic relationship is a complementary relationship. In this form of relationship, the difference between the two parties in a superior/inferior relationship is increased or escalated to a dangerous degree.[8]

Interdependence exists in both types of schismogenic relationships in that both parties define their existence according to the other. Symmetrical schismogenesis is a game of comparison that can annihilate the world in the case of the arms race. Each country must work to gain supremacy in order to maintain its identity as a world power. In the case of complementary schismogenesis, such as an oppressor/oppressed relationship, each party gains its identity by its position in the relationship. Without an oppressed, there can be no oppressor and vice versa. If nothing is done to alter these schismogenic relationships, the problem often gets worse. The interdependence gets out of hand and escalates to a dangerous level. The contention that schismogenic relationships are interdependent systems that have gotten out of control announces that the human is not an isolated creature, but lives in a context where interdependence of persons is a natural phenomenon. Yet this interdependence can become a danger to both parties, as in the case of an arms race or oppressed/oppressor relationship.

Another problem involving interdependence arises when individuals within the interdependent system totally forsake their own identity outside the relational system. At that point, a collectivism develops that ignores the individual variations and characteristics of all people involved. Arthur Koestler describes revolutionary ethics where the collective end justifies the means. The collective cause of the revolution subsumes all other considerations. The individual is no longer an important consideration. In Koestler's *Darkness at Noon,* Ivanov is an interrogator of an individual who has become an enemy of the party. Ivanov states:

> 'The principle that the end justifies the means is and remains the only rule of political ethics; anything else is just vague chatter and melts away between one's fingers'. . . . 'There are only two conceptions of human ethics, and they are at opposite poles. One of them is Christian and humane, declares the individual to be sacrosanct, and asserts that the rules of arithmetic are not to be applied to human units. The other starts from the basic principle that a collective aim justifies all means, and not only allows, but demands, that the individual should in every way be subordinated and sacrificed to the community — which may dispose of it as an experimental rabbit or a sacrificial lamb. . . . Whoever is burdened with power and responsibility finds out on the first occasion that he has to choose; and he is fatally driven to the second alternative.'[9]

The problem that Koestler describes is that an individual may begin to see people as so interdependently intertwined that individual characteristics are forgotten or ignored. Interdependence can then become the problem of collectivism, in which people define themselves so much by the collective cause that their own individuality is lost.

The Community of Otherness

Chapter Seven, Commitment or Narcissism?, revealed the limitations of a self-centered individualistic orientation. The previous material in this chapter has announced that interdependence can manifest itself in collectivism. Thus, there needs to be a constructive alternative that is neither a self-centered individualism nor a collectivism where the parts have become so interdependent that individual uniqueness is lost. Some of the representatives of the historic peace churches recognized that individual uniqueness should not be forgotten. One person stated that a constructive concept of nonviolent peacemaking requires an interreligious orientation that embraces all cultures. Another individual pointed to the need to affirm individual uniqueness. Yet another peacemaker stated that the human must learn to care for the other. No one has the right to downgrade another person; the concern should be to build her up in order to encourage her individual potential. These comments clearly reveal a need to affirm the individual uniqueness of persons. This reveals a need for a being-in-the-world that is neither individualistic nor collectivistic, but embraces a concern for all humanity while supporting individual uniqueness. One individual described this dilemma by stating that in any community structure, there are two types of tyranny. When no rules exist, then a strong charismatic leader often tyrannizes the group; yet on the other hand, rules that are too strict can oppress people. The problem is that both individualism and collectivism can tyrannize; neither system for participating in life activities is really adequate.

Dietrich Bonhoeffer, in *Life Together,* refers to the problem of having both community and independence of thought. Speaking with a commitment to Christ, Bonhoeffer says: "Where Christ bids me to maintain fellowship for the sake of love, I will maintain it. Where his truth enjoins me to dissolve a fellowship for love's sake, there I will dissolve it, despite all the protests of my human love."[10] Bonhoeffer has pointed to a significant problem that a person may encounter as he works for nonviolent peace and change. There may be times that a nonviolent peacemaker disagrees with a group decision so vehemently that he must have the independence to stand alone and not follow the group, even at the expense of dissolving a fellowship. For there are some disagreements that cannot be easily swept aside. A person may not be able to conform to the community decision. Not all conflicts are solvable. At times the parties in disagreement may walk their own separate paths, particularly if the conflict in question is a value confrontation. Thus, the human needs to affirm a way of being-in-the-world that does not merely affirm the importance of community right or wrong, or an individualistic self-centered orientation.

> *Collectivism* suppresses the unique wonder of the individual person, whether in ruthless totalitarianism and racism or in seemingly benign philosophies that ask us to abandon freedom and personal dignity for the sake of gaining a happy manipulated society. *Individualism* destroys the sustaining ties of human affection, whether in competitive economic ideologies or in the protests of rebels who disdain the processes of community life.[11]

The human needs to have the courage to be a participating part of a community and maintain her own individual being. One must correlate two aspects of being, association with others and separateness. The human needs to accept the dialectical nature of existence that requires the bringing together of both the courage to be a part of the larger community and the courage to be oneself. Human existence is a call to life that resides between the extremes of forsaking one's identity for the community and asserting individuality to the extent that one's connection to others in the world community is forgotten.

Maurice Friedman calls the way of being that is neither individualism nor collectivism a "community of otherness." In that community the human is called to offer a dual response to living. He confirms the uniqueness and differentness of persons and he also affirms the importance of community, which has a meaning larger than the individual. Friedman says that the person must be willing to risk and venture into a life of communal authenticity and personal growth. This sense of community means that the individual is significant and vital, but not the total reality. Reality includes the world community as well as individual. The community of otherness does not avoid conflict; it recognizes it as the way of bringing forth issues that need attention. The voice of the other is heard, not ignored when it questions the goals of the collective. Friedman states that the community of otherness can only grow as individuals challenge the positions held by persons and/or the community when disagreement occurs, and also affirm the importance of individual persons and community. The uniqueness of the other must be affirmed and the need to follow one's own vision must be supported. Through confirming the other and working to resolve differences and attempting to understand other views the community is strengthened.[12]

Perhaps the goal of a nonviolent peacemaker is a koinonia community. "The New Testament rarely uses the term 'people' or 'nation';

in its place is the Greek word koinonia. This is the term for the most intimate human relationship possible."[13] James Jones in "The Practice of Peoplehood," says that koinonia neither stresses individualism nor uniformity, but attempts to transcend both: " . . . the uniqueness of each member is preserved and cherished but each freely lays down his life in the service of others."[14] Perhaps the community of otherness, like koinonia, is the most intimate of all human relationships in that people commit themselves to a global community without losing their own uniqueness — for there is nothing an individual can give a community that is more sacred than her own unique way of being in and seeing the world. The community may challenge an individual's vision and vice versa, but in the community of otherness, the person is confirmed.

Chapter Nine

Confronting in Dialogue

The representatives of the historic peace churches described a particular way of addressing another, whether friend or opponent, in which the human voices his view while openly attempting to understand the other's perception of an event. One individual said that a nonviolent peacemaker should not allow the other to manipulate her in a conversation. She should speak with clarity and compassion without desiring to dominate the other. Both parties should be free to accept or reject the comments of the other. Another individual said that a nonviolent peacemaker needs to be nonabrasive with his fellows and at the same time openly state his opinion. The previous comments reveal a mode of relating to another in conflict that is much different than a debate between opponents. In a debate, one person's view is eventually thought to be superior to another's. In dialogical confrontation, the answer to a conflict emerges "between" the conflicting parties. This answer may or may not be what one of the parties originally proposed. A person needs to voice her opinion and openly attempt to understand the other's viewpoint. In this exchange, a person may come to agree with the opponent and change her viewpoint on an issue. However, even if a person does not accept the opponent's view, she still does not seek to dominate him or her.

Resolving a conflict in dialogue requires the recognition of the humanity of both parties in the conflict. This method of dealing with conflict is an initial step toward dialogue. An individual voices his view while attempting to understand the other's perspective, which invites an exchange between two or more individuals to occur. Dialogue can be invited by one party, but it can only be given life by the efforts of all parties in conflict.

Another element of dialogue is pointed to by some other representatives of the historic peace churches. One individual stated that in conflict the nonviolent peacemaker needs to accept and respect the other, even though they may disagree. However, as the nonviolent peacemaker respects her opponent, the nonviolent peacemaker expresses her viewpoint; she does not remain quiet. One individual said that in communicating with another, he attempted to manifest a

> . . . willingness to be present, to state my position, to expose myself in an attempt to be persuasive, but not to be detrimental in the decision making, that is not to exercise a kind of force that is necessary to make the decisions come out my way, or even the conflict to be resolved my way.

In dialogue, each person is allowed to voice his view and finds that action affirmed by his opponent even in disagreement. An individual may attempt to persuade the other, but he does not use the kind of force that would ignore the other's right to a particular viewpoint.

Commitment Yet Openness

The above comments point to two important components in a dialogical encounter. First, an individual needs to stand her own ground, while being open to the other's view. A person is open to change, but only as he becomes convinced that another solution to a conflict is more acceptable. In dialogue as both parties stand firm in openness to the other, the final resolution may be a combination of the opposing views or one party may persuade the other to affirm the perspective he once opposed, or a previously unrecognized solution may emerge from the dialogue. Second, as a person stands her own ground in dialogue, she affirms the other's right to the same privilege. An individual may disagree with the other's view of a situation, but his right to hold that view is supported.

Martin Buber referred to dialogue as the unity of contraries, in that the human must stand her own ground yet be open to the other in a single movement. The human must walk with his partner in dialogue on a "narrow ridge" between two extremes: (1) refusing to attempt to understand the other's perspective of a situation, and (2) forsaking one's own ground and blindly following the other's opinion. A listener who does not attempt to hear her partner's view is closed to different views. Only material that is compatible with his previous expectations and past prejudices is comprehended. The opposite problem is the listener who is too easily directed by her partner. She has no ground of her own and quickly accepts the other's comments and opinions. According to Buber, to invite a dialogical encounter, the human must give up both extremes. An individual must participate in a "holy insecurity" that does not cling to either extreme. The person walks a narrow ridge in a holy insecurity that requires him to stand between the extremes of stubbornly standing his own ground and blindly following his partner's direction.[1]

The walking of the narrow ridge between standing one's ground and being open to the other's perception of the world is revealed through the actions of Martin Buber on September 27, 1953. At that time, Martin Buber was awarded the Peace Prize of the German Book Trade in Paulskirche, Frankfurt, Germany. Martin Buber's acceptance speech was entitled "Genuine Dialogue and the Possibilities of Peace." When Buber gave his speech to the German audience, less than a decade had passed since the Jewish people had been so horribly deprived of their humanity. As Buber accepted his award, he openly stated his heartfelt belief that no previous historical event had ever been so systematically executed and organized as the cruelty the German people had inflicted upon his people. He said:

> I, who am one of those who remained alive, have only in a formal sense a common humanity with those who took part in this action. They have so radically removed themselves from the human sphere, so transposed themselves into a sphere of monstrous inhumanity inaccessible to my conception, that not even hatred, much less an overcoming of hatred, was able to arise in me. And what am I that I could here presume to "forgive"![2]

Martin Buber stood his own ground and delivered a message to his German audience that he had neither forgotten nor forgiven the actions of the German people.

Buber could have ended his speech at this point. He could have stood his ground without the accompanying movement of being open to the other. He could have rejected the difficult task of walking the narrow ridge between the extremes of a closed mind and acceptance of what many in the audience had implicitly and/or explicitly sanctioned. But Buber was not a man to address another with either a closed focus or an optimistic naivete. He stood his ground and allowed his own voice to be heard; and in an accompanying dual movement, he opened himself to establishing a common link between himself and his German audience. The following quotation, from later in Buber's address, dramatically reveals his openness to the other.

When I think of the German people of the days of Auschwitz and Treblinka, I behold, first of all, the great many who knew that the monstrous event was taking place and did not oppose it. But my heart, which is acquainted with the weakness of men, refuses to condemn my neighbour for not prevailing upon himself to become a martyr. Next there emerged before me the mass of those who remained ignorant of what was withheld from the German public, and who did not try to discover what reality lay behind the rumours which were circulating. When I have these men in mind, I am gripped by the thought of the anxiety, likewise well known to me, of the human creature before a truth which he fears he cannot face. But finally there appears before me, from reliable reports, some who have become as familiar to me by sight, action, and voice as if they were friends, those who refused to carry out the orders and suffered death or put themselves to death, and those who learned what was taking place and opposed it and were put to death, or those who learned what was taking place and because they could do nothing to stop it killed themselves. I see these men very near before me in that especial intimacy which binds us at times to the dead and to them alone. Reverence and love for these Germans now fills my heart.[3]

Martin Buber was firm and clear in his speech. He engaged in an authentic dialogue of walking a narrow ridge in the realm of holy insecurity, in which he neither failed to listen nor forsook his own ground.

The dual motion of standing one's ground and attempting to confirm the other's humanity by being open to his view of the world, even in confrontation, was basic to Buber's understanding of human life. He viewed persons as separate, yet was able to simultaneously invite human contact and understanding. Martin Buber contended that before a person can enter into "relation" with another, there must be "distance" between the parties; each partner in the dialogue needs to be confirmed as a unique and individual being.

Genuine conversation, like every genuine fulfillment of relation between men, means acceptance of otherness. This means that although one may desire to influence the other and to lead him to share in one's relation to truth, one accepts and confirms him in his being this particular man made in this particular way. One wishes him to have a different relation to one's own truth in accordance with his individuality. The manipulator of propaganda and suggestion, in contrast, wishes to make use of men. He relates to men not as independently other beings but as to things, things moreover with which he will never enter into relation and which he is eager to rob of their distance.[4]

The task of the human is to confirm the individual uniqueness of her partner whether in friendly conversation or heated argument and conflict. An individual may still attempt to change her partner's viewpoint, but in dialogue the other's individual uniqueness and humanity is recognized. However, the uniqueness of each human is sometimes forgotten, even when agreement occurs. For instance, one may convince another that one's view of the world is correct and then be annoyed by the particular manner in which the other acts on that view of existence. The human often forgets that the other will give his own unique expression to the carrying out of a task. One must be careful not to ask the other to give up her distance and become a carbon copy of herself in action. The goal is to confirm the other and, if necessary, to also wrestle with opposing views. Demand to carry out issues of common agreement in the same way denies the other his common, yet unique humanity.

Buber's emphasis on the uniqueness of the person does not mean that he affirms an ethic of self-realization. An individual who seeks self-realization is often primarily concerned about engaging in activities that will promote her own personal growth and fulfillment of her potential. However, there are times when a person must engage in an activity that may limit his potential. The historical situation both offers opportunities and limits one's options. As the nonviolent peacemaker meets the historical situation, it is apparent that the goal of peace and justice has not been achieved for all persons. A nonviolent peacemaker may limit her income or choose a vocation that will allow her to promote the goals of peace. These decisions may limit her options and not allow her to fulfill other facets of her potential. But even as a person answers a need of the historical situation, she does so in her own personally unique manner. This is not the ethic of self-realization, but an affirmation of personal uniqueness as an individual responds to the need of the historical moment.

Martin Buber demonstrated the importance of confirming the other even while confronting him in argument. When Buber was invited to speak at a university, he stayed with an old gentleman who still visualized each moment as a new beginning. The last few years had been war years and this sensitive and perceptive man had seen and felt the difficulty of those times. But he was an open man, even in the midst of the pain he felt all about him in that warring climate. During his stay at the old man's home, Martin Buber worked on the preface to one of his books. The statement dealt with religious faith and evoked the name of God a number of times. Buber's host wished to hear the preface, and Buber gladly obliged him. The old gentleman sat quietly and listened eagerly to Buber's material. But as Buber continued to use the name of God time after time, the eyes of his host became flared and his voice grew angry as he addressed Buber.

> 'How can you bring yourself to say "God" time after time? How can
> you expect that your readers will take the word in the sense in which
> you wish it be taken? What you mean by the name of God is some-
> thing above all human grasp and comprehension, but in speaking
> about it you have lowered it to human conceptualization. What
> word of human speech is so misused, so defiled, so desecrated as
> this! All the innocent blood that has been shed for it has robbed it
> of its radiance. All the injustice that it has been used to cover has ef-
> faced its features.'[5]

Buber responded by saying that indeed humans had used the
word of God to justify their own authority, to kill, to maim, and to
dehumanize others. But the fact that the word has been misused does
not mean that a person should be silent until the word is redeemed.
"We cannot cleanse the word of "God" and we cannot make it whole;
but defiled and mutilated as it is, we can raise it from the ground and
set it over an hour of great care.'"[6] After these two men had argued in-
tensely with one another, the " . . . old man stood up, came over to
me, laid his hand on my shoulder and spoke: 'Let us be friends.' The
conversation was completed."[7] The old gentleman did not persuade
Buber to use another term and from the story it is not certain that the
host agreed with Martin Buber's reasoning for evoking the name of
God so frequently in his essay. The reader cannot determine if one
man changed the other's view, but one outcome is clear—each man's
common, yet unique humanity was confirmed by the other in the confrontation. Confirming the other does not ensure that the other will
adopt one's point of view, but it does increase one's chances of having
another opportunity to try.

Confrontation and Reconciliation

Martin Buber viewed each human as unique; he contended that a
person in dialogue should affirm her partner's uniqueness. Throughout his thought, Buber recognized that distance and difference between humans is a natural part of the living process. But Buber did not
believe a person was personally whole if he did not bring his personal
uniqueness into relation with others. Personal wholeness requires
uniqueness of person meeting with his fellows.

A lack of personal wholeness is present when an individual does
not have the courage to stand her own ground and bring her own
unique response into relation with another. Many times a person is
afraid of what others may think of his personal and unique response
to a situation. He then escapes taking responsibility for his own

unique response or personal ground of understanding by avoiding meeting or entering into relation with the other in one of two ways. First, an individual may leave his ground and blindly follow the other's understanding and perception of an event, thereby escaping responsibility for his own unique response. The other's concern becomes his direction. For example, a person could leave his own ground and only feel the other's pain or hurt. This apparent helping of another could be detrimental to what the other may need. An individual may need to become more independent and not rely so much on his fellows. If the human stands his own ground, he has a perspective on the situation that is unique and different, which may help in the solving of the problem. The second way a person can avoid responsibility is by "protecting" her unique viewpoint or ground by holding others at a distance. This defensive maneuver shields her from various viewpoints. Thus, she is locked in on her own opinion, unable to receive stimulation that could confirm, or change her perception.

The human must find an option between blindly giving himself to others and distancing himself from the rest of humanity. In both cases, the person does not bring his unique response to the relationship. He avoids really meeting the other by establishing a technique of groundless self-giving or self-protecting defensiveness. People often do not stand their ground in order to avoid conflict. One may attempt to console the other without presenting one's own view, which may do an injustice to the other. A person cannot gain another perspective on the situation if the other is always forsaking his ground for the safety of a consoling statement. Conflict sometimes needs to be overtly acknowledged in order for the possibility of dialogue or an authentic relationship to unfold.

One needs to be responsible to the other by voicing her unique response in the relation. An individual does not give up his personally unique way of viewing the world. One meets one's partner on one's own ground and confirms her by being open to her view, even in argument. The human has the responsibility in a dialogical encounter to engage in this dual movement with the other.

As one responds toward the other in the relation, he "turns toward" his partner and attempts to experience "the other side of the dialogue." The other person is allowed to be fully present in the relationship. According to Buber, one should attempt to see through the eyes of his partner, in order to learn what the other's perception of a particular happening may be. Responsibility means hearing one's partner in the concrete moment or immediate situation and then responding from the depth of his being. This does not mean that an individual simply "spills his guts" to another. The situation must call for how much he should reveal.

Buber's attention to the concrete situation means that different situations require their own particular responses. No one can tell another how she should respond before she enters the situation, according to Buber's view of responsibility in dialogue. As each person brings his uniqueness to the situation, his response will naturally be different than another person's answer to that happening. As each person offers her own unique response to a situation, some responses will be more appropriate than others. Some individuals may listen to the situation and the other more carefully. Then they answer the particular need of the situation that is announced with their own unique response. Thus, for Buber, responsibility means standing one's own ground and being open to the other *and* the situation. Each person and each situation makes its own demands. The listener then answers, but with his own personally unique response.[8]

The importance of responding to the other in the unique situation requires an authentic listening to and answering of the concrete moment. There is no technique or formula for such responsibility; it is the bringing of one's unique response to answer an address from a person and/or situation. Martin Buber states:

> Genuine responsibility exists only where there is real responding. . . . Moreover, nothing that he believed he possessed as always available would help him, no knowledge and no technique, no system, and no programme; for now he would have to do with what cannot be classified, with concretion itself. . . . We respond to the moment, but at the same time we respond on its behalf, we answer for it. A newly created concrete reality has been laid in our arms; we answer for it. A dog has looked at you, you answer for its glance, a child has clutched your hand, you answer for its touch, a host of men moves about you, you answer for their need.[9]

As the human stands her own ground and opens herself to establish contact with the other, she does not have the safety of a technique or formula that tells her how to respond. The human merely has the responsibility to answer with her own response to the address she has received.

A nonviolent peacemaker attempting to stand his own ground and remain open to the other will act differently as various situations address him. Different situations call for their own particular response from a nonviolent peacemaker which he then attempts to provide in his own unique fashion. But as nonviolent peacemakers question how to respond to opponents or what specific action they should take, they should remain responsible to the life-calling that guides their behavior. Maurice Friedman described the human's responsibility to respond to a situation that addresses him with his whole being through his own life-calling.

> Our uniqueness is our personal vocation, our life-calling that is discovered when we are called out by life to become 'ourselves' in responding. We must respond to this call from where we are, and where we are is never social nor merely individual but uniquely personal. We need to be confirmed by others. Our very sense of ourselves only comes in our meeting with others. We do not begin as isolated consciousness. Yet, through this confirmation we can grow to the strength of Socrates, who said, 'I respect you, Athenians. But I will obey the god and not you.' Socrates expressed his responsibility to his fellow Athenians precisely in opposing them. Responsibility means to respond, and a genuine response is the response of the whole person.[10]

When an individual is addressed by the historical situation of the world, she may discover her life-calling as she responds. A nonviolent peacemaker is addressed or called out by life to offer an alternative to the violent pattern that typifies the historical situation. This means that for a nonviolent peacemaker, each unique response to a conflict happening is guided by the address that calls for a nonviolent alternative. Thus, as a nonviolent peacemaker seeks to offer his personally unique response to the problems that confront the global community, the specific manner of response is bound to the situation but is completed in the spirit of his own responsibility of offering the option of nonviolent peacemaking.

There are several reasons for so much variance in responses to the historical situation. First, not all people even attend to what is happening in their family, group, or global community. They do not listen to potential warning signs. Thus, their response is oblivious of the address. Second, some individuals hear the address of the historical situation differently. Each person is unique; therefore, each person's interpretation of the historical situation is different. The nonviolent peacemaker can only give herself to the task of answering the call she has heard. To be personally responsible an individual must offer her unique response to the call of the historical moment. Maurice Friedman contends that true guilt is a failure to respond to one's personal responsibility; it is a guilt from responding too little, too late, or without one's entire being.[11] To avoid personal guilt, the nonviolent peacemaker needs to respond to problems that address him in the means of nonviolent peacemaking.

Paul Keller, in the editorial "A Song to Be Heard," states that nonviolent peacemakers must work for social justice, if the song of a nonviolent alternative is to be heard. But, as the peacemakers attempt to bring themselves to this task, they need to affirm their own calling of responsibility. The quest is to respond with an orientation that offers a clear alternative to violence.

> This is no time, it seems to me, for those who hold a pacifist position to lose their nerve. We need now, more than ever before, to be clearheaded and strong in reaffirming our rejection of violence. . . . But if we take a strong stand against violence, we must take an equally strong stand against the social injustice that depends on it and that inspires more of it.[12]

To deal with social injustice from a nonviolent peacemaking stance requires nonviolent peacemakers to have responsibility or a willingness to respond in a manner congruent with what they affirm. This responsibility requires them to stand their own ground of nonviolent peacemaking and confirm the other by attending to the other's viewpoint even in confrontation.

Perhaps the nonviolent peacemaker in conflict is most responsible to his calling when she responds to another in the dual motion of not only confirming but caring for the opponent as she stands her own ground and allows her own voice to be heard. One person hoped his hands were gentle hands that worked to shape, not destroy the other. One individual stated that nonviolent peacemaking requires caring for the other. And when one confronts the other, this attitude needs to be present in order to prevent conflict and separation from continuing for a long duration. Another person said that nonviolent peacemaking requires a positive redemptive type of influence, in which one's reaction is not determined by the other's response. One peacemaker said that he lived with ambiguity. He recognized the necessity to confront evil and oppression, but he also desired to seek reconciliation. Another individual said that nonviolent peacemaking requires an individual to assertively articulate her position on violence, without dominating the other. Yet another individual stated that nonviolent peacemaking involves a nonviolent opposition to violence, but that act of redemption for the opponent is always present. One of the representatives of the historic peace churches said he was intrigued with David Augsburger's concept of conflict as care-fronting. Augsburger says that "care-fronting is the key to effective relationships. It's the way to communicate with impact and respect, with truth and love."[13] The above statements are pointing to the importance of standing one's ground and confronting, yet being open to the other's humanity and caring for him. One peacemaker described an incident that reveals caring confrontation.

> My father told me of an incident where one man cursed another
> . . . and forbade him ever to speak to him again. Across the years the
> cursed man would speak when he had the opportunity, while the
> other man avoided him in every way he could. Finally the man got sick
> and the man who was not ever to speak again went to the woodpile of
> the sick man and cut wood for awhile. Then he took an armload into
> the house and sat down by the bed of the sick man and began to talk in
> a friendly manner with him. From this a lasting friendship grew. As
> my father told this story he closed by saying, 'I know this is a true story
> for I am the man that cut the wood.'

The manner in which the above person's father handled the situation did
not allow the other man to intimidate him or control him. He spoke at
every opportunity, even though he was told not to do so, thereby confronting his opponent. But he also attempted to be open to the other and
to care about him in a manner that was not only attitudinal, but visible in
his actions.

As a nonviolent peacemaker attempts to confront another in a caring fashion, she may even risk her own life. Roland Bainton, in *Christian Attitudes Toward War and Peace,* relates the following incident. A
German pacifist, Hans de Boer, went to Kenya determined to talk to the
leaders of the Mau Mau. As he arrived in the country, he consulted with
an American Quaker who had been working to maintain a line of
trustful communication with the Mau Mau for twenty years. The
Quaker's advice to de Boer was that he should not walk into the area of
the Mau Mau stronghold, if he feared for his life. De Boer did not heed
the advice. He walked unarmed into the Mau Mau territory, a feat that
the Quakers had not even attempted. The Mau Mau were so impressed
by this man's courage that he not only was not harmed, but one of the
Mau Mau leaders invited him to have a conference. De Boer found that
freedom and land rights, not a desire to destroy all whites, were the basis
for the Mau Mau conflict with authorities.[14] The actions of de Boer may
seem foolhardy and dangerous. But, if personal communication between opponents is not established, then individuals may see bloodshed
as the only resolution to the conflict. De Boer confronted the Mau Mau
by walking into a dangerous battlefield unarmed. Yet he simultaneously
demonstrated his caring, as he listened to the Mau Mau's understanding
of the situation.

The importance of caring confrontation is that a person may
vehemently disagree with his opponent, while affirming the opponent's
right to voice his perspective on a situation. Confrontation occurs
within a framework of caring for the other's humanity and rights.

As previously stated, dialogue requires an individual to understand the other's world and simultaneously stand her own ground. Indeed, the test of this dual movement of dialogue for a nonviolent peacemaker may be the moment of caring confrontation. As Paul Keller has often stated in conversations and lectures, the true test of dialogue is in conflict, not in casual conversation.

Dialogue with another in a caring confrontation focuses attention on the issue of disagreement without forgetting the importance of others. This mode of confrontation may open the door for an eventual beneficial reconciliation. Through the announcement of one's own voice and caring for the other, the possibility of reconciliation may be open after the conflict encounter. Dale Brown states the importance of confrontation in conjunction with reconciliation.

> An easy peace without confrontation is often achieved by keeping the lid on basic injustice. Confrontation apart from the context of reconciliation eventuates in an unending cycle of retaliation. Only peace achieved through confrontation, involving grace and judgment, love and justice, will suffice.[15]

Caring confrontation of the opponent can embrace a dialogical movement of standing one's own ground and voicing one's own opinion and simultaneously being open to the other's view, even in disagreement. It is possible to confront the issue at hand and still attempt to care for one's opponent; it is this dual movement which may ultimately lead to reconciliation, rather than retaliation.

Chapter Ten

The Dialogue of Peace

When attempting to resolve human conflict, the representatives of the historic peace churches contended that the goal should be mutual resolution. Their concern was to conclude the conflict in a manner that benefitted both parties in a just fashion. One person stated:

> . . . my attitude toward that [resolution of conflict] is that I can't stop searching for ways that would make it possible to be in conflict and at the same time . . . contribute to each other's mutual growth. I think as soon as the goal of mutual growth is dropped on the scale of values, so that it no longer is the foremost value, then those things . . . [that are contrary to] pacifism are likely to make themselves known. And so my search is for ways in which conflict . . . can be engaged in without irreparable damage to either of the parties involved. That means that I'm not content with any ways of dealing with conflict that reward one person and penalize another.

One individual said that as he attempts to resolve conflict happenings, his goal is to arrive at a mutual resolution that embraces both equality and justice. Another individual stated that his concern is to promote a mutual resolution in an open atmosphere between opponents.

Some of the peacemakers offered comments that revealed domination of the other as a conflict resolution tactic that is incompatible with the achievement of mutual resolution. One person stated that the tendency of the human to exploit another needs to be altered. Another individual said that violence can be used psychologically and physically against those who cannot always defend themselves, such as children and the elderly. Societal structures need to be changed, in order to halt these situations. Any atmosphere that does not allow persons to freely differ is ultimately unhealthy. One person said that drastic differences between the affluent and the poor will probably lead to an outburst of physical violence, unless it is soon corrected. The world's resources will have to be more equitably shared. One individual stated that she thought it was counter-productive to continually seek to dominate others. She also pointed to the importance of recognizing the opponent's humanity. Another person stressed the importance of this same theme. But, he stated that the human is often unable to acknowledge the humanity of the conflicting party. An individual may be too concerned about his own security.

> . . . it's the seizing of the attempt to guarantee his own security and his own status in the world and his own future that actually destroys and undermines it [the possibility of reconciliation] . . . there's a kind of grasping and drive to control one's destiny, or to have the power to control it as fully as possible. Since that can never be obtained in the nature of things. . . . it's an insatiable drive. And no matter how much one accumulates in the way of wealth, physical power, economic power, or any form of security . . . it's never sufficient. . . . we're all in competition for each other because our drive to gain security throws us in competition with each other . . . which is basically destructive. . . . I don't know as I want to say it's inherent but that there's something inherent in the human situation that results in this kind of destructive competitiveness.

It is important to be sensitive to the needs of others, which requires a willingness to negotiate openly rather than to force a resolution by using domineering power tactics. The human often seeks to dominate the other through a variety of means. However, the above statements describe the importance of mutual resolution. Thus, a nonviolent peacemaker needs to reject the temptation to use domination of another as a method of conflict resolution. The main tenet of nonviolent action is to act in a way that the needs of both parties are met at least somewhat adequately in a non/win-lose situation.

Seeking Humanness in Conflict

The importance of not relying on domination as a method of conflict resolution is pointed to by Brown and Keller, in their manuscript on conflict resolution. They state two hypotheses about human conflict: First, in destructive conflict, the other person's self-esteem and values are threatened, and she is forced to give more than she receives in the resolution. Second, in constructive conflict, the other is confirmed, his values are acknowledged, and the benefits of the resolution do not outweigh the costs for either party.[1] Brown and Keller announce the importance of supporting each party's self-esteem in a nondominating atmosphere, in order to enhance the possibility of a beneficial resolution of the conflict situation. Morton Deutsch, in *The Resolution of Conflict: Constructive and Destructive Processes,* also describes the importance of mutual resolution in a nondominating environment.

> Any attempt to introduce a change in the existing relationship between two parties is more likely to be accepted if each expects some net gain from the change than if either side expects that the other side will gain at its expense. . . . [This method of resolution] underlies the approach to intergroup conflict of Gandhi, Martin Luther King, and many other proponents of nonviolence.[2]

Clearly, a lasting and productive resolution of conflict most often does not result in winners and losers, but works toward a mutually beneficial conclusion to the conflict. To achieve a lasting resolution a nonviolent peacemaker should work for mutual resolution of a conflict, and forego the temptation to utilize domination as a method or goal in a conflict encounter. To attempt to dominate another ignores the importance of compatibility of means and ends.

The importance of seeking a relationship with others that is not based on domination is revealed by Gandhi's attempt to voice his recognition of the untouchables in India. Gandhi considered the doctrine of untouchability the greatest curse on Hinduism, because it implied a superior/inferior relationship, which Gandhi thought was demeaning to both parties. "To convince people of the injustice of untouchability he had recourse to many ways of persuasion. For instance he repeatedly told people that we have no right to speak against foreign domination till we rid ourselves of the domination of our own people."[3] But Gandhi did not stop at merely describing domination of the untouchables as wrong. He called them by a different name, "Harijan," which meant people or children of God. He asked the Harijans to live with him in his Ashram as members of one large family with people from all castes in India. He also adopted a girl who was Harijan, and he encouraged and supported members of other castes to marry Harijans. Gandhi was concerned with the human dignity of individuals, which a dominating relationship ignores. " . . . For Gandhi neither birth nor occupation essentially differentiates one man from another, because it is the one and the same human nature that is participated in by every human being which brings with it human rights and human dignity."[4]

To work from a base of domination in a conflict situation provides a person with an advantage that must be constantly maintained. The oppressor must again and again assert her superiority in the relationship. And when the oppressed reject the role of the dominated, a violent confrontation may be the result. Sometimes the situation appears so bleak that the oppressed may strike out blindly and violently against domination. Saul Bernstein, in *Alternatives to Violence,* offered an interesting statement regarding the Watts riots in the 1960s that further illuminates this theme. Bernstein said that one group investigated the cost and time required to travel from the Watts area to downtown Los Angeles, where most of the jobs and hospitals were available. They found that the time varied from one to two hours each way and the round trip cost almost one dollar. In addition, the travelers were required to make three or four changes from one bus line to another with each of these requiring waiting time. Not all the places were work could be found were accessible with public transportation from the Watts area. Bernstein concludes:

> No great imagination is required to grasp what it must mean to a Negro in Watts to undertake these complex trips before and after a hard day's work. Unless the job is well paid, his net income could easily be less than he would receive from public welfare. At least as disturbing would be the experience of taking an ill family member to the hospital by a succession of buses.[5]

This one annoyance regarding public transportation does not totally explain the Watts riots. But it does point to the notion that the black person in the Watts area lived under difficult circumstances that emphasized his subordination to the decisions of those in power. Perhaps violence seemed the only way to restore their own power as people in a powerless and dominated situation.

The need to ventilate anger and restore one's ignored humanity in a dominated atmosphere is not an uncommon reaction to oppression. Rollo May contends that Frantz Fanon, who authored *The Wretched of the Earth,* clearly regarded violence as an acceptable mode of action in a dominated situation. Violence is then used to reinstate one's personal dignity. However, it is the need to rebel against domination that makes domination only a temporary victory that may eventuate in additional conflict and physical confrontation. It is often merely temporary containment of the conflict. Domination of another is incompatible with mutual resolution and may even foster heightened violence at a later date. Thus, a person needs to search out methods other than domination, if she desires a resolution that may benefit both parties and will not later result in violence.

The reverse problem concerns what the nonviolent peacemaker should do if he is the dominated or oppressed party. An interpretation based on the nonviolent peacemaking of Fanon's work points to the answer.

> When Fanon's books were reviewed by a pacifist Quaker, the reviewer remarked that wherever Fanon uses the word violence, one could read nonviolence and the meaning would be the same. In other words, Fanon is talking of human dignity, the birth and growth of consciousness, integrity of relationships.[6]

If the nonviolent peacemaker is part of the dominated party, then nonviolent peacemaking in the form of protest and/or resistance can be an avenue that will allow one to assert her human dignity without destroying the other. Human dignity, as Fanon stated, should not be denied. The nonviolent peacemaker accepts this premise; only the means of implementation are dissimilar. Thus, a means for resolving conflict that embraces a tactic of domination ignores the humanity of the other and will eventually lead the oppressed to reassert his human dignity in one manner or another.

The concern of the nonviolent peacemaker is to find the appropriate and compatible means of achieving a peaceful and just resolution of a conflict situation. Evan Thomas provides an interesting way of looking at the means-end problem. He contends that the human is accustomed to thinking in terms of ends rather than means. The problem with a perceived end is that it is seldom the true end, in the sense of finality; rather, it is usually just a step on a long and uncertain journey. Thus, Thomas says that means or methods should be a person's concern because the ultimate end is forever unknown. The human has demonstrated what concern over ends can achieve in the form of domination and oppression. Perhaps it is time to follow the unknown path of means that are compatible with the goal of peace and justice.[7] The nonviolent peacemaker's search to find means for resolving conflict that are compatible with his ultimate quest leads him to affirm methods of resolution that acknowledge the human dignity of each person in the conflict encounter.

Means of encountering another that recognize the opponent's humanness versus means that ignore the other's humanity are described by Martin Buber. He articulated two primary attitudes or relations between humans, which reveal the nature of relationships that either confirm or ignore the other's human significance. He considered the most confirming human relationship an "I-Thou" encounter. He contended that an "I-It" relationship objectifies the other without confirming her common, yet unique, humanity. An I-Thou encounter recognizes the other's humanity, while an I-It relationship objectifies the other. The nonviolent peacemaker must then decide which means of relating to another is compatible with her end goal of a peaceful world community. An I-Thou relation points to a means of encountering an opponent that is compatible with the end goal of peace for every human.

An I-It encounter with another tends to ignore the other's humanity. This mode of relation is typified by a subject-object orientation. The other always remains a stranger; he is merely an object to be used, manipulated, and experienced. What he says is subjectively interpreted within the listener's own view of the world. An I-It orientation is egocentric or ethnocentric — the meaning of the other's world is judged from one's own value system.[8] For example, if an individual went to a foreign land and judged the cultural practices from her own viewpoint, she would never actually meet the people of that land. She would only see objects that she interpreted from her own subjective point of view, without attempting to understand their natural cultural climate.

An I-It relation is not necessarily evil; sometimes it aids the human in using the world in a pragmatic and necessary way. When information processing is the primary concern of communication, an I-It relation may be necessary. In this exchange of technical information, the other often becomes an object that remains unknown; relationship between partners is not vital to the exchange. But in a conflict situation, both information and relationship between persons are necessary components in the encounter. To forget one's relationship to the other is to potentially ignore the other's humanity. This may lead to the resolution of the issue at hand, but create another conflict situation because the other's personhood has been ignored or oppressed. This form of resolution is indeed a win/lose method of dealing with conflict. One may win the issue at hand, but lose his partner by using methods of resolution that ignore personhood. An I-It orientation is potentially destructive as a conflict strategy, in that the opponent is viewed as an object that must be manipulated into agreement with one's own view of an issue.

An I-It encounter is referred to as a monological relation with the other, in which the goal is to enhance oneself or to win the issue in debate while relationship is ignored. Reuel Howe says that:

> . . . in monologue a person is concerned only for himself and that, in his view, others exist to serve and confirm him. . . . His communication is parasitical because he is really interested in others and

values them only according to the feelings they produce in him. He .
. . seeks confirmation of himself, is afraid of personal encounter,
and tolerates only agreement with himself and his ideas. And he is
uncreative because his word is a closed, not open, one; that is, he
seeks to present his own meaning as final and ultimate.[9]

Martin Buber says that a monological encounter is characterized by
speaking in such a way that the words strike their mark in the sharpest
manner possible. The other's reaction to the bluntness of the uncaring
tone is not considered. Often monologue occurs when there is no need
to communicate with, hear from, or influence the other; the concern is
to reinforce one's self-image. The person who is addressed becomes interchangeable with any person capable of confirming one's self-
expectations. In a monological conversation the other is not significant; only his role as a confirmer is of importance to the speaker.[10]
This mode of relating to another human being is closely associated
with propaganda. The primary motive is to win a person over to the
cause and accumulate more members. The individual member is de-
personalized into a category. Only quantity not the quality of relationship between persons is the concern.

Joan Bondurant, in *Conquest of Violence,* says that in recent
years, some nonviolent tactics have been used in Gandhi's name that
are not at all representative of his satyagraha campaigns. These
tactics reveal a monological approach to nonviolent protest and resistance.

> The words duragraha and satyagraha are compounds sharing the
> sanskrit noun *agraha,* 'firm grasping.' The prefix *dur* (used in com-
> pound for *dus*) denotes 'difficult,' and one meaning of duragraha is
> 'bias.' In the refinement of language for describing techniques for
> social action, duragraha serves to distinguish those techniques in
> which the use of harrassment obscures or precludes supportive acts
> aimed at winning over the opponent.[11]

When fundamental change is needed, duragraha is ineffective. It
presses forward its demands in a self-righteous and arrogant manner
that leads to rigid opposition and even more oppressive reaction. The
technique of duragraha concentrates on winning the issue or cause and
the relationship between the parties in conflict is forgotten. This approach to nonviolence is monological, because an individual deter-
mines for herself the correct course of action without taking her opponents view into consideration. The opponent is treated as an object;
who she is and what she believes are only obstacles to overcome in
order to fulfill one's own wishes.

Dialogue Between Opponents

Chapter Nine described two components of dialogue, both of which are dual movements. First, an individual needs to stand his own ground while confirming the other, by attending to the other's view of the conflict situation. Second, a person needs to voice her perspective while affirming her opponent's right to this same privilege. Dialogue embodies an additional characteristic that further distinguishes it from monologue—the ontological reality of the "between." As previously stated, a monological conversation is typified by a person stubbornly clinging to a subjective view of a conflict happening without considering his opponent's view. In dialogue, both parties meet in a relation in which the result of that meeting does not reside *in* either party, but emerges "between" them. Buber says of dialogue:

> . . . no matter whether spoken or silent—[dialogue happens] where each of the participants really has in mind the other or others in their present and particular being and turns to them with the intention of establishing a living mutual relation between himself and them. . . . [However the distinction between monologue and dialogue] must not be confused with the contrast between 'egoism' and 'moralism' conceived by some moralists. I know people who are absorbed in 'social activity' and have never spoken from being to being with a fellow-man. I know others who have no personal relation except to their enemies, but stand in such a relation to them that it is the enemies' fault if the relation does not flourish into one of dialogue.[12]

Martin Buber is stating the importance of dialogue occurring "between" two parties standing their own ground in openness. But he is also pointing to the notion that social concern does not ensure concern for one's opponent, as in the case of monologue or duragraha. He also reveals that dialogue with one's opponent is an authentic possibility.

Again, the significant element of Buber's dialogue is the "between." As one encounters another in dialogue in the dual movement of firmness in conviction yet openness to the other, the answer to a conflict or confrontation is not the property of either party; rather it emerges "between" them. In *Between Man and Man,* Buber states that the fundamental concern of human life is not in any man or woman, collective or thing. Real living emerges "between" a person and what she encounters.

> 'Between' is not an auxiliary construction, but the real place and bearer or what happens between men . . . . what is essential does not take place in each of the participants or in a neutral world

which includes the two and all other things; but it takes place between them in the most precise sense, as it were in a dimension which is accessible only to them both.[13]

The "between" is conceptually important to a peaceful resolution because in this dialogical view of conflict neither party possesses the sole truth to any argument. The truth emerges "between" both parties. This does not necessarily mean a compromise occurs; rather through the dual movement of standing one's ground in openness, changes in one or both of the viewpoints may occur. Thus, the final resolution is the product of two parties. By attempting to "experience the other side" of the relationship a person gains new ideas; and by standing her own ground until she might be persuaded otherwise, she gives the opponent a chance to encounter her view of the situation. A dialogical meeting with an opponent recognizes the importance of both parties in the relationship, which promotes the possibility of an answer emerging "between" them. The emergent answer "between" opponents may reveal that no resolution is possible at a particular moment. But, if dialogue has occurred, then the atmosphere of affirmation inherent in dialogue may encourage the parties to at least consider talking again about the issue of contention.

The importance of a resolution methodology that attends to the answer to a conflict happening that may emerge "between" the opponents is that the resolution requires both parties to be present and the resolution is the property of the relationship, not one party in the conflict. This is revealed by Gandhi's method of satyagraha. It provides an excellent exemplification of the dual movement and the "between" of dialogue. Gandhi attempted to invite a resolution that incorporated the views of both parties in conflict. He never knew the answer to a conflict happening before he entered dialogue with his opponent. The end or the answer that emerged "between" opponents was never predetermined.

> The objective of satyagraha is to win victory over the conflict situation — to discover further truths and to persuade the opponent. . . .
> Holding to the truth means holding to what the satyagrahi believes to be the truth until he is dissuaded from that position or part of it.
> . . . Perhaps the most characteristic quality of satyagraha is the flexibility in ends which an emphasis on means implies. . . . His [Satyagrahi] dogma — if such a thing can be alleged of him — lies in adherence to a means, to a technique, which has . . . specific moral elements at its base. But what action in these terms may mean — what it may lead to as a social, or political, or individual end — is highly unpredictable.[14]

Gandhi's holding to the truth until he is dissuaded from his position is similar to the dual movement of dialogue — standing one's own ground yet being open to the other view of the situation. And Gandhi's flexibility of ends points to the fact that he did not possess a preconceived answer to a situation before he entered the conflict situation with his opponent. Dialogically this means that the final resolution must emerge "between" the two conflicting parties, incorporating some, not necessarily equal, elements of each opposing position. Thus, satyagraha is a method of resolving conflict that relies on dialogue between opponents in an authentic effort to affirm the humanity of all participants in a dispute. As Joan Bondurant stated, Gandhi's contribution to nonviolence was his concern for the well-being of the opponent and a goal of mutual triumph for both oppressor and oppressed.[15] Indeed, these are the goals of dialogue as a person allows his own voice to be heard by his opponent.

Gandhi's Satyagraha and Buber's Dialogue are not techniques or strategies of manipulation that seek victory for one's own side without regard for the other. Any methodology of resolution that ultimately seeks to gain a superior position without concern for the opponent's welfare is contrary to both satyagraha and dialogue. Also, any technique that is based in a preconceived answer to a conflict is unlike the methods proposed by Buber and Gandhi. Finally, any conflict resolution methodology that does not recognize the need for the final resolution to incorporate both parties and belong to neither is at odds with the goals of satyagraha and dialogue. Thus, any conflict methodology that does affirm the above statements has some commonality with the general aims of Gandhi's Satyagraha and Buber's Dialogue. But the concern for the humanity of all people tends to place satyagraha and dialogue in a special category for the nonviolent peacemaker. Both Buber and Gandhi were involved in intense conflict situations. The oppression of the Jewish and Indian people provided much of the ground that nourished the thought of these two men. The results of their own relations with others seem to be embodied in their approaches.

Gandhi and Buber point in a similar direction. They both attempted to describe ways of relating that allow a person to voice her own opinion and in a dual motion, attempt to understand the other's view. However, one must recognize that Buber and Gandhi did not always agree on the means for promoting change in conflict situations. This is revealed in the Buber-Gandhi letters. For example, Gandhi contended that satyagraha could have been effectively used by the Jewish people to resist Nazi tyranny. But Buber contended that Gandhi did not understand the historical differences between the British and German modes of oppression.[16] Disagreements such as these cannot be ignored, but the importance of how the work of these two men contribute to one another is of even greater significance to nonviolent peacemaking. V. V. Ramana Murti, in an article "Buber's Dialogue and Gandhi's Satyagraha," says that the main course of history will remain unaffected by the possibilities of genuine dialogue, unless the means for conducting it are more clearly formulated.

> *Satyagraha* is the answer to the basic question that is inherent in the *Dialogue*. The methods of *satyagraha* such as nonviolent non-cooperation, genuine self-sacrifice, and voluntary suffering fulfill the great end of the *dialogue*. Nor is the likeness between Buber's doctrine and Gandhi's principle confined to the techniques in an unmistakable unity of spirit between Buber's *dialogue* and Gandhi's *satyagraha*. Both of them supremely recognize the divine mission of human existence. The *Dialogue* seeks a fundamental transformation of I-It relationship into an I-Thou relationship. . . . The same truth is also reiterated by the *satyagraha* which offers the 'soul force' as an alternative to the 'brute force' in the resolution of human conflicts. Its doctrine of non-violence is now the only way to save civilization from the threat of non-existence.[17]

Murti contends that Gandhi's Satyagraha provides a concrete exemplification of Buber's Dialogue. Thus, it is quite possible for a nonviolent peacemaker to give life to Buber's dialogical principles. The human can invite dialogue with his opponent as he lends his own uniqueness to the following of four general guidelines. First, nonviolent peacemakers need to stand their own ground and be open to the other's view of the situation. Second, they need to voice their own opinion while affirming their opponent's right to state his or her view. These two guidelines for resolving conflict reveal caring for both oppressor and oppressed. The humanity of each opponent is affirmed, as each is given the opportunity to state her own view of a conflict happening. Third, pre-established answers to a conflict situation need to be rejected. A durable resolution involves all parties; it cannot be accomplished in solitude. Fourth, the final resolution is not the property of any one person. No one possesses the right decision or the superior resolution; it emerges "between" opponents. The resolution is the property of the dialogue, to which both parties have given their efforts. The last two guidelines do not ensure resolution. But if an answer is discovered, the chances of reconciliation are certainly enhanced, since both parties fulfilled constructive and necessary roles in the resolution.

Dialogue is an important component in an effort to resolve conflict within the framework of nonviolent peacemaking. Both dialogue and nonviolent peacemaking work to open and maintain communication with the other. Even in confrontation, the human who engages in dialogue confirms the other and the human who accepts a nonviolent peacemaking orientation to violence affirms the sanctity of the other's life. A merging of dialogue and nonviolent peacemaking does not answer all conflict problems. But these two orientations can work together as a dual force that can invite the other to meet in conversation and attend to the resolution answer that emerges "between" them. Perhaps no answer may be the temporary result that emerges, but confirmation of the other through dialogue and affirmation of the other's right to live through nonviolent peacemaking may at least promote an atmosphere that invites and encourages the other to re-enter the negotiating arena.

Epilogue:
Hope for Tomorrow

Part One, Living Within Peacemaking Limits, pointed to some of the limitations that a peacemaker may operate within as she accepts nonviolent peacemaking as a life style. Nonviolent peacemaking is applicable to all levels of living, because violence to the other occurs in all aspects of life. The ignoring glance of disconfirmation or the categorization of the other can forget the opponent's humanity. As the nonviolent peacemaker works for the end of peace and social justice, he sees the need to use means that are compatible with that goal. Thus, he attempts to care for both oppressor and oppressed. Finally, she is not naive about the other's response to her loving action; violence or even death may be the reward from the other. The hope is that the escalating nature of violence can be halted on the interpersonal as well as the international level. To stop the escalating nature of violence requires a conscious commitment to nonviolent peacemaking, not only on an international level, but in daily interpersonal interaction.

Part Two, Peacemaking in a Violent World, described the importance of affirming an image of the human that recognizes the existence of both good and evil. The nonviolent peacemaker needs to invite the goodness of the other to unfold with full knowledge that he may meet an antithetical response. Human conflict is inevitable. Sometimes a person's own value system naturally leads her into conflict; and occasionally an individual must consciously elicit conflict through a nonviolent protest. However, some nonviolent peacemakers may view conflict and power as destructive or evil and attempt to avoid their use. Power and conflict need not be viewed as inherently evil; they can be manifestations of human passion or energy that only need a constructive outlet. Nonviolent peacemaking in protest and resistance can provide a constructive direction for power and conflict. Thus, what appears to be an evil may be only a manifestation of human energy that needs to be directed in a positive fashion. The nonviolent peacemaker needs to affirm power and conflict as potentially constructive avenues for human energy when given direction through nonviolent peacemaking. Power and conflict need to be united with the desire for a peaceful world of justice for all humans, in which nonviolence is accepted as the only compatible means to achieve the desired goal of peace. Nonviolent peacemaking without the energy or passion manifested in power and conflict can be avoidance or even cowardice. The passion of power and conflict without love and compassion for the other may promote the destruction of the oppressed and/or oppressor, not the liberation of both parties. Thus, a nonviolent peacemaking image of the human requires the recognition of the needed union of good and potential evil, in the process of inviting a just and peaceful existence for all parties in conflict.

Part Three, The Radical Commitment, announced the importance of a person foregoing the quest for direct or indirect self-fulfillment in order to be accessible to the ongoing happenings and needs of the world. For the nonviolent peacemaker, the radical commitment could potentially promote the development of a world community that is an alternative to either collectivism or individualism. The nonviolent peacemaker needs to work to create a community of otherness, where individual uniqueness is affirmed in the larger quest toward a peaceful and just world community.

A radical commitment recognizes the compatibility of dialogue and nonviolent peacemaking. Gandhi's satyagraha provides a concrete exemplification of the dialogical principle used in nonviolent peacemaking. A nonviolent peacemaking approach to the resolution of conflict often rests on the possibility of the human entering into dialogue with her opponent, as each voices her opinion and recognizes the humanity of the other. Maurice Friedman states:

> Sometimes that dialogue can only mean standing one's ground in opposition to him, witnessing for what one believes in the face of his hostile reaction of it. Yet it can never mean being unconcerned for how he sees it or careless of the validity of his standing where he does. We must confirm him even as we oppose him, not in his 'error' but in his right to oppose us, in his existence as a human being whom we value even in opposing.[1]

The way of dialogue and peacemaking does not guarantee success. But it reveals the importance of confirming the other and recognizing his humanity as one opposes him. Possibly, as long as the humanity of the other is recognized, means for resolving conflict that limit the humanness of one or both parties will be rejected as tactics for conflict resolution.

This book has attempted to reveal that an alternative to violence on an interpersonal as well as international level is a conceptual and liveable possibility. This work is based in a trust that violence is not the way to peaceful and just global society. One peacemaker stated:

> . . . I don't think that the only force in the world is violent. There's
> no doubt about the amount of violence. But someone has to say
> that's not the way it is to be, and has to say out of trust that there is
> a force beyond violence which is active within the world and which
> ultimately will prove to be the more powerful.

There is no guarantee that nonviolent peacemaking will always be effective; there is only a basic trust that it is a means for resolving conflict that may in the final analysis contribute to the mutual growth of human beings.

Perhaps the peacemaker's hope for tomorrow rests in a basic trust that an alternative to violence exists, and that an alternative to conflict avoidance is also available. Nonviolent peacemaking rejects both violence and avoidance as appropriate means for resolving human conflict. The extremes of violence and avoidance are easily understood in the western world, because of its dichotomous nature. Often it is difficult to see alternatives between extremes. Communist/capitalist, dove/hawk, proletariat/bourgeoisie, or radical/status quo are but a few of the dichotomous statements that are prevalent modes of thought. Sometimes it seems that any suggested alternative to the presently accepted extremes is often reluctantly acknowledged. Humans tend to place phenomena in opposition to one another and exclude a third alternative. Martin Buber, in an essay "Hope for This Hour," stated:

> The human world is today, as never before, split into two camps,
> each of which understands the other as the embodiment of
> falsehood and itself as the embodiment of truth. Often in history, to
> be sure, national groups and religious associations have stood in so
> radical an opposition that the one side denied and condemned the
> other in its innermost existence. Now, however, it is the human
> population of our planet generally that is so divided, and with rare
> exceptions this division is everywhere seen as a necessity of existence
> in this world hour. He who makes himself an exception is suspected
> and or ridiculed by both sides. Each side has assumed monopoly of
> the sun light and has plunged its antagonist into night, and each side
> demands that you decide between day and night.[2]

Buber goes on to say that this division is caused by a basic mistrust and a fear to enter dialogue. Indeed, both violence and avoidance of conflict are often the result of a basic mistrust that is rooted in the fear of meeting the other in dialogue. Violence denies the other's humanity and right to live. Avoidance of conflict does not recognize that life is by nature sometimes conflict generating. This book has contended that one can affirm a basic trust in an alternative to the extremes of violence and avoidance, which consists of dialogue inclusive of nonviolent peacemaking. The nonviolent peacemaker recognizes the sanctity of life while she works for a dialogical resolution "between" opponents. He is open to the other's view while he announces his own voice clearly and firmly. Martin Buber has stated that: "The hope for this hour depends on the renewal of dialogical immediacy between men."[3] Perhaps, more correctly, the hope for tomorrow may rely on the trust that an alternative to the extremes of violence and avoidance does exist. Perhaps non-violent peacemaking along with human dialogue is a needed alternative in the task of resolving conflict "between" humans.

Notes

Chapter One

1. Kenneth Brown, "Updating Brethren Values: Rule Pacifism," *Brethren Life and Thought,* XII (Summer, 1967), p. 21.

2. Kenneth Brown, pp. 22-23.

3. Eric Mosbacher, trans., *The Bound Man and Other Stories,* by Ilse Aichinger (New York: The Noonday Press, Inc., 1956), p. 6.

4. Gene Sharp, *Power and Struggle, Part One of The Politics of Nonviolent Action* (Boston: Porter Sargent Publishers, 1973), p. 88.

5. Sharp, p. 89.

6. Paul Watzlawick, Janet Beavin and Don Jackson, *Pragmatics of Human Communication: A Study of Interactional Patterns, Pathologies, and Paradoxes* (New York: W.W. Norton and Company, Inc., 1967), p. 86.

7. Martin Luther King, Jr. "Let Us Be Dissatisfied," *Gandhi Marg,* XII, No. 3 (1968), p. 229.

8. King, Jr., p. 219.

9. James W. Douglass, *The Non-Violent Cross: A Theology of Revolution and Peace* (New York: MacMillan Publishing Co., Inc., 1973), p. 29.

10. Robert Jay Lifton, "The 'Gook Syndrome' and 'Numbed Warfare,'" *Peacemaking: A Guide to Conflict Resolution for Individuals, Groups, and Nations,* ed. Barbara Stanford (New York: Bantam Books, Inc., 1976), p. 232.

11. Robert D. Nye, *Conflict Among Humans: Some Basic Psychological and Social Psychological Considerations* (New York: Springer Publishing Co., 1973), pp. 9-15, 105-106.

Chapter Two

1. Joan V. Bondurant, *Conquest of Violence: The Gandhian Philosophy of Conflict* (Berkeley: University of California Press, 1971), p. 8.

2. Erik H. Erikson, *Gandhi's Truth: On the Origins of Militant Nonviolence* (New York: W.W. Norton and Company, Inc., 1969), p. 412.

3. Erikson, p. 411.

4. Bondurant, pp. 21-22.

5. Maurice Friedman, *Touchstones of Reality: Existential Trust and the Community of Peace* (New York: E.P. Dutton and Co., Inc., 1974), pp. 21-29.

6. Ronald Duncan, ed., *Gandhi: Selected Writings* (New York: Harper and Row Publishers, 1972), p. 42.

7. Duncan, p. 276.

8. Thomas Merton, "The Meaning of Satyagraha," *Gandhi Marg,* X, No. 2, (1966), p. 111.

9. Gordon Shull, "The Pilgrimage of an Ex-Pacifist," *Brethren Life and Thought,* V, No. 2 (1960), pp. 18-19.

10. Dale W. Brown, *Brethren and Pacifism* (Elgin, Illinois; Brethren Press, 1960), pp. 52-53.

11. Paul Watzlawick, John H. Weakland, and Richard Fisch, *Change Principles of Problem Formation and Problem Resolution* (New York: W.W. Norton and Company, Inc., 1974), pp. 1-28.

12. Rollo May, *Power and Innocence: A Search for the Sources of Violence* (New York: Dell Publishing Company, Inc., 1972), p. 220.

13. May, *Power,* pp. 221-222.

14. Maurice Friedman, "Martin Luther King: The Modern Job," *Gandhi Marg,* XII, No. 3 (1968), p. 232.

15. Friedman, "King," pp. 230-239.

Chapter Three

1. G.H.C. Macgregor, *The New Testament Basis of Pacifism* (Nyack, New York: Fellowship, 1959), p. 117.

2. Brown, *Brethren,* p. 51.

3. Brown, *Brethren,* p. 54.

4. Abraham J. Muste, *Not By Might/Christianity: The Way to Human Decency and of Holy Disobedience* (New York: Garland Publishing Inc., 1971), p. 84-85.

5. May, *Power,* pp. 63-64.

6. C. Wayne Zunkel, "Violence and Nonviolence," *Six Papers on Peace: A Symposium* (Elgin: Church of the Brethren General Board, 1969), p. 52.

7. Pitirim A. Sorokin, "The Powers of Creative Unselfish Love," *New Knowledge in Human Values,* ed. Abraham H. Maslow (Chicago: Henry Regnery Company, 1959), pp. 10-11.

8. May, *Power,* pp. 48-49.

9. Albert Camus, "Neither Victims Nor Executioners," *The Human Dialogue: Perspectives on Communication,* ed. Floyd W. Mat-

son and Ashley Montagu (New York: The Free Press, 1967), p. 305.

10. John Howard Yoder, *The Politics of Jesus* (Grand Rapids: William B. Eerdmans Publishing Company, 1972), pp. 240-243.

11. Jacques Ellul, *Violence: Reflections from a Christian Perspective* (New York: The Seabury Press, 1969), p. 173.

12. Dietrich Bonhoeffer, *Cost of Discipleship* (New York: Mac-Millan Publishing Co., Inc., 1975), p. 53.

13. Dietrich Bonhoeffer, *Letters and Papers from Prison* (London: Collins Clear-Type Press, 1970), p. 182.

14. Viktor E. Frankl, *Man's Search for Meaning: An Introduction to Logotherapy* (New York: Pocket Books, 1974), p. 121.

15. Thomas Merton, *Faith and Violence: Christian Teaching and Christian Practice* (Notre Dame, Indiana: Universty of Notre Dame Press, 1968), pp. 75-84.

Chapter Four

1. Maurice Friedman, *The Hidden Human Image* (New York: Dell Publishing Co., Inc., 1974), p. 4.

2. Center for the Study of Social Policy, *Changing Images of Man,* (Menlo Park, California: Stanford Research Institute, 1974), pp. 1-20.

3. Erich Fromm, *The Anatomy of Human Destructiveness* (Greenwich, Connecticut: Fawcett Publications, Inc., 1975), p. 22.

4. Fromm, p. 36.

5. Fromm, pp. 521-528.

6. James Strachey, trans., *Civilization and Its Discontents,* by Sigmund Freud (New York: W.W. Norton and Company, Inc., 1962), p. 92.

7. Marjorie Kerr Wilson, trans., *On Agression,* by Konrad Lorenz (New York: Harcourt, Brace and Wilson, Inc., 1966), pp. 236-274.

8. Robert Ardrey, *African Genesis: A Personal Investigation into the Animal Origins and Nature of Man* (Forge Village, Massachusetts: Murray Printing Company, 1961), pp. 28-29.

9. Ardrey, p. 357.

10. Abraham H. Maslow, *The Farther Reaches of Human Nature* (New York: The Viking Press, 1973), p. 15.

11. Maslow, *Farther,* p. 15.

12. Viktor E. Frankl, *Man's Search for Meaning: An Introduction to Logotherapy* (New York: Pocket Books, 1974), pp. 212-213.

13. Martin Luther King, Jr., "Pilgrimage to Nonviolence," *Fellowship* (May, 1976), p. 9.

Chapter Five

1. William Robert Miller, *Nonviolence: A Christian Interpretation* (New York: Schocken Books, 1972), p. 34.

2. Barbara Stanford, "Conflict," *Peacemaking: A Guide to Conflict Resolution for Individuals, Groups and Nations,* ed. Barbara Stanford (New York: Bantam Books, Inc., 1976), pp. 15-18.

3. Richard Walton, *Interpersonal Peacemaking: Confrontations and Third Party Consultation* (Reading, Massachusetts: Addison-Wesley Publishing Co., 1969), p. 5.

4. George R. Bach and Peter Wyden, *The Intimate Enemy: How to Fight Fair in Love and Marriage* (New York: Avon Books, 1973), p. 17.

5. Charles Chatfield, *For Peace and Justice: Pacifism in America 1914-1941* (Boston: Beacon Press, 1973), p. 69.

6. Chatfield, p. 87.

7. Emmert F. Bittinger, *Heritage and Promise: Perspectives on the Church of the Brethren* (Elgin, Illinois: The Brethren Press, 1970), p. 38.

8. Roger E. Sappington, *Courageous Prophet: Chapters From the Life of John Kline* (Elgin, Illinois: The Brethren Press, 1964), p. 109.

9. Sappington, pp. 110-111.

10. Aubrey Hodes, *Martin Buber: An Intimate Portrait* (New York: Viking Press, 1971), p. 165.

11. Fromm, p. 75.

12. Martin Buber, *Between Man and Man* (New York: MacMillan Company, 1972), p. 82.

Chapter Six

1. Richard B. Gregg, *The Power of Nonviolence* (2nd ed.; New York: Schocken Books, 1971), p. 63.

2. Leroy H. Pelton, *The Psychology of Nonviolence* (New York: Pargamon Press Inc., 1974), p. 133.

3. Pelton, pp. 113-114.

4. Joan V. Bondurant, "Force, Violence and the Innocent Dilemma," *Gandhi Marg,* 9, No. 3 (July, 1965), p. 185.

5. Horace Alexander, "Ends and Means in the Pursuit of Peace," *Gandhi Marg,* 11, No. 2 (April, 1967), p. 134.

6. Theodore Roszak, "Gandhi and Churchill: A Dialogue on

Power," *Peacemaking; A Guide to Conflict Resolution for Individuals, Groups, and Nations,* ed. Barbara Stanford (New York: Bantam Books, Inc., 1976), p. 404.

7. Roszak, p. 404.

8. Maurice Friedman, trans., *A Believing Humanism: Gleanings,* by Martin Buber (New York: Simon and Schuster, 1969), p. 45.

9. Martin Luther King, Jr., "Let Us Be Dissatisfied!" *Gandhi Marg,* 12, No. 3, (July, 1968), p. 222.

10. Johan Galtung, "Pacifism from a Sociological Point of View," *Journal of Conflict Resolution,* III, No. 1 (1959), p. 73.

11. A.J. Muste, *Of Holy Disobedience* (Lebanon, Pennsylvania: Sowers Printing Company, 1973), pp. 31-32.

12. Henry Thoreau, *On the Duty of Civil Disobedience* (London: Housmans, 1976), p. 9.

Chapter Seven

1. Gregory Rochlin, *Man's Aggression: The Defense of the Self* (New York: Dell Publishing Co., Inc., 1973), pp. 201-202.

2. Frederick S. Perls, *In and Out the Garbage Pail* (New York: Bantam Books, Inc., 1972), p. i.

3. Walter Tubbs, "Beyond Perls," *Journal of Humanistic Psychology,* 12, No. 2 (Fall, 1972), p. 5.

4. Maurice Friedman, "Aiming at the Self: The Paradox of Encounter and the Human Potential Movement," *Journal of Humanistic Psychology,* 16, No. 2 (Spring, 1976), p. 6.

5. Brewster Smith, "On Self-Actualization: A Transambivalent Examination of a Focal Theme in Maslow's Psychology," *Journal of Humanistic Psychology,* 13, No. 2 (Spring, 1973), p. 21.

6. Smith, p. 30.

7. Smith, p. 30.

8. Maurice Friedman, *To Deny Our Nothingness: Contemporary Images of Man* (New York: Dell Publishing Co., Inc., 1967), p. 30.

9. Maurice Friedman, *The Hidden Human Image* (New York: Dell Publishing Co., Inc., 1974), p. 276.

10. Viktor E. Frankl, *The Will to Meaning: Foundations and Applications of Logotherapy* (New York: New American Library, Inc., 1969), p. 38.

11. Viktor E. Frankl, *The Doctor and the Soul: From Psychotherapy to Logotherapy* (New York: Random House, Inc., 1973), pp. 26-62.

12. Letter from Ray Wagner, September 19, 1977.

13. *Martin Buber,* "Elements of the Interhuman," *Bridges Not Walls: A Book About Interpersonal Communication* 2nd ed., ed. John Stewart (Reading, Massachusetts: Addison-Wesley Publishing Company, 1977), p. 283.

14. Maurice Friedman, *Touchstones of Reality: Existential Trust and the Community of Peace* (New York: E.P. Dutton and Co., Inc., 1974), p. 322.

Chapter Eight

1. Martin Luther King, Jr., "Vietnam and the Struggle for Human Rights," *War and the Christian Conscience: From Augustine to Martin Luther King, Jr.,* ed. Albert Marrin (Chicago: Henry Regnery Company, 1971), pp. 303-304.

2. King, p. 304.

3. George Lakey, *Strategy for Living Revolution* (San Francisco: W.H. Freeman and Company, 1973), p. 201.

4. Charles R. Joy, ed., *Albert Schweitzer: An Anthology* (Boston: Beacon Press, 1967), pp. 259-262.

5. Thomas Merton, *Thomas Merton on Peace* (New York: McCall Publishing Company, 1971), p. 62.

6. Merton, pp. 63-66.

7. Rollo May, "Gregory Bateson and Humanistic Psychology," *Journal of Humanistic Psychology,* 16, No. 4 (Fall, 1976), pp. 38-39.

8. Gregory Bateson, *Steps to an Ecology of Mind* (New York: Ballantine Books, 1974), pp. 68-72.

9. Daphne Hardy, trans., *Darkness at Noon,* by Arthur Koestler (New York: Bantam Books, 1972), pp. 127-128.

10. John W. Doberstein, trans., *Life Together,* by Dietrich Bonhoeffer (New York: Harper & Row, Publishers, 1976), p. 35.

11. J. Edward Carothers, and others, ed., *To Love or to Perish: The Technological Crisis and the Churches* (New York: Friendship Press, 1972), p. 26.

12. Friedman, *Hidden,* pp. 358-371.

13. James W. Jones, "The Practice of Peoplehood," *Sojourners* (May, 1977), p. 8.

14. Jones, p. 9.

Chapter Nine

1. Maurice S. Friedman, *Martin Buber: The Life of Dialogue* (Chicago: University of Chicago Press, 1976), p. 3.

2. Maurice S. Friedman, trans., *Pointing the Way: Collected Essays,* by Martin Buber (New York: Harper and Brothers, 1957), p. 232.

3. Buber, *Pointing,* p. 233.

4. Friedman, *Life,* pp. 81-82.

5. Martin Buber, *Meetings,* ed. Maurice Friedman (La Salle, Illinois: Open Court Publishing Company, 1973), p. 50.

6. Buber, *Meetings,* p. 51.

7. Buber, *Meetings,* pp. 51-52.

8. Maurice Friedman, "The Bases of Buber's Ethics," *The Philosophy of Martin Buber,* eds. Paul Arthur Schilpp and Maurice Friedman (La Salle, Illinois: Open Court Publishing Company, 1967), pp. 171-172.

9. Martin Buber, *Between Man and Man* (New York: MacMillan Company, 1972), pp. 16-17.

10. Maurice Friedman, "Dialogue and the Unique in Humanistic Psychology," *Journal of Humanistic Psychology,* 12, No. 2, (Fall, 1972), pp. 15-16.

11. Maurice Friedman, "Existential Psychotherapy and the Image of Man," *Journal of Humanistic Psychology,* IV, No. 2, (Fall, 1964), p. 115.

12. Paul Keller, "A Song to Be Heard," *Messenger,* 125, No. 3 (March, 1976), p. 25.

13. David W. Augsburger, *The Love-Fight* (Harrisonburg, Virginia: Choice Books, 1973), p. 3.

14. Roland H. Bainton, *Christian Attitudes Toward War and Peace: A Historical Survey and Critical Re-evalution* (New York: Abingdon Press, 1960), pp. 265-266.

15. Dale W. Brown, *The Christian Revolutionary* (Grand Rapids: William B. Eerdmans Publishing Company, 1971), pp. 129-130.

Chapter Ten

1. Charles T. Brown and Paul W. Keller, "Strategies of Constructive and Destructive Conflict" (Unpublished Manuscript, 1977).

2. Morton Deutsch, *The Resolution of Conflict: Constructive and Destructive Processes* (New Haven: Yale University Press, 1973), p. 99.

3. V. Tellis-Nayak, "Gandhi on the Dignity of the Human Person," *Gandhi Marg,* 7, No. 1 (1963), p. 50.

4. Tellis-Nayak, p. 52.

5. Saul Bernstein, *Alternatives to Violence: Alienated Youth and Riots, Race and Poverty* (New York: Association Press, 1969), p. 30.

6. Rollo May, *Power and Innocence: A Search for the Sources of Violence* (New York: Dell Publishing Co., Inc. 1976), p. 192.

7. Evan W. Thomas, "Ends and Means," *The Radical "No": The Correspondence and Writings of Evan Thomas on War,* ed. Charles Chatfield (New York: Garland Publishing, Inc., 1974), pp. 275-278.

8. Ronald Gregor Smith, trans., *I and Thou,* by Martin Buber, (2nd ed.; New York: Charles Scribner's Sons, 1958), pp. 31-32.

9. Reuel L. Howe, *The Miracle of Dialogue* (New York: The Seabury Press, 1963), p. 36.

10. Buber, *Between,* pp. 19-20.

11. Joan V. Bondurant, *Conquest of Violence: The Gandhian Philosophy of Conflict* (Berkeley: University of California Press, 1971), p. viii.

12. Buber, *Between,* pp. 19-20.

13. Buber, *Between,* pp. 203-204.

14. Bondurant, pp. 33-34.

15. Bondurant, p. 119.

16. V.V. Ramana Murti, "Buber's Dialogue and Gandhi's Satyagraha," *Journal of the History of Ideas,* 24, No. 4 (1968), pp. 605-607.

17. Murti, p. 611.

Epilogue

1. Maurice Friedman, *The Hidden Human Image* (New York: Dell Publishing Co, Inc., 1974), p. 368.

2. Martin Buber, "Hope for This Hour," *The Human Dialogue: Perspectives on Communication,* eds. Floyd W. Matson and Ashley Montagu (New York: The Free Press, 1967), pp. 306-307.

3. Buber, "Hope," p. 312

Bibliography

Alexander, Horace. "Ends and Means in the Pursuit of Peace," *Gandhi Marg,* 11, No. 2 (April, 1967).

Ardrey, Robert. *African Genesis: A Personal Investigation into the Animal Origins and Nature of Man.* Forge Village, Massachusetts: Murray Printing Company, 1961.

Augsburger, David W. *The Love-Fight.* Harrisonburg, Virginia: Choice Books, 1973.

Bach, George R. and Peter Wyden. *The Intimate Enemy: How to Fight Fair in Love and Marriage.* New York: Avon Books, 1973.

Bainton, Roland H. *Christian Attitudes Toward War and Peace: A Historical Survey and Critical Re-evaluation.* New York: Abingdon Press, 1960.

Barrett, William. *Irrational Man: A Study of Existential Philosophy.* New York: Doubleday and Company, Inc., 1962.

Bateson, Gregory. *Steps to an Ecology of Mind.* New York: Ballantine Books, 1974.

Bernstein, Saul. *Alternatives to Violence: Alienated Youth and Riots, Race, and Poverty.* New York: Association Press, 1969.

Bittinger, Emmert F. *Heritage and Promise: Perspectives on the Church of the Brethren.* Elgin Illinois: The Brethren Press, 1970.

Bondurant, Joan V. *Conquest of Violence: The Gandhian Philosophy of Conflict.* Berkeley: University of California Press, 1971.

_____. "Force, Violence and the Innocent Dilemma," *Gandhi Marg,* 9, No. 3 (July, 1965), 181-186.

Bonhoeffer, Dietrich. *Cost of Discipleship.* New York: MacMillan Publishing Co., Inc., 1975.

_____. *Letters and Papers from Prison.* London: Collins Clear-Type Press, 1970.

Brown, Charles T. and Paul W. Keller. *Monologue to Dialogue: An*

Exploration of Interpersonal Communication. Englewood Cliffs, New Jersey: Prentice-Hall, Inc., 1973.

_____. "Strategies of Constructive and Destructive Conflict." Unpublished manuscript, 1977.

Brown, Dale W. *Brethren and Pacifism.* Elgin, Illinois: Brethren Press, 1960.

_____. *The Christian Revolutionary.* Grand Rapids: William B. Eerdmans Publishing Company, 1971.

Brown, Kenneth. "Updating Brethren Values: Rule-Pacifism," *Brethren Life and Thought,* XII (Summer, 1967), 18-23.

Buber, Martin. *Between Man and Man.* New York: MacMillan Company, 1972.

_____. *Good and Evil: Two Interpretations.* New York: Charles Scribner's Sons, 1953.

_____. *Meetings,* ed. Maurice Friedman. LaSalle, Illinois: Open Court Publishing Company, 1973.

Carothers, J. Edward and others, ed. *To Love or to Perish: The Technological Crisis and the Churches.* New York: Friendship Press, 1972.

Center for the Study of Social Policy. *Changing Images of Man.* Menlo Park, California: Stanford Research Institute, 1974.

Chatfield, Charles. *For Peace and Justice: Pacifism in America 1914-1941.* Boston: Beacon Press, 1973.

_____, ed. *The Radical "No": The Correspondence and Writings of Evan Thomas on War.* New York: Garland Publishing, Inc., 1974.

Dellinger, Dave. *Revolutionary Nonviolence.* Garden City, New York: Doubleday and Company, Inc., 1971.

Deutsch, Morton. *The Resolution of Conflict: Constructive and Destructive Processes.* New Haven: Yale University Press, 1973.

DeVito, Joseph A., ed. *Language: Concepts and Processes.* Englewood Cliffs, New Jersey: Prentice-Hall, Inc., 1973.

Diwakar, R. R. "Satyagraha: A New Way of Life and a New Technique for Social Change," *Gandhi Marg,* 13, No. 4 (October, 1969), 16-25.

Doberstein, John W., trans. *Life Together,* by Dietrich Bonhoeffer.

New York: Harper and Row, Publishers, 1976.

Douglass, James W. *The Non-Violent Cross: A Theology of Revolution and Peace.* New York: MacMillan Publishing Co., Inc., 1973.

Driver, Peter M. "Toward an Ethnology of Human Conflict: A Review," *Journal of Conflict Resolution,* XI, No. 3 (1967).

Duncan, Ronald, ed. *Gandhi: Selected Writings.* New York: Harper and Row Publishers, 1972.

Ellul, Jacques. *Violence: Reflections from a Christian Perspective.* New York: The Seabury Press, 1969.

Erikson, Erik H. *Gandhi's Truth: On the Origins of Militant Nonviolence.* New York: W. W. Norton and Company, Inc., 1969.

Frankl, Viktor E. *The Doctor and the Soul: From Psychotherapy to Logotherapy.* New York: Random House, Inc., 1973.

_____. *Man's Search for Meaning: An Introduction to Logotherapy.* New York: Pocket Books, 1974.

_____. "On Logotherapy and Existential Analysis," *American Journal of Psychoanalysis,* 18, No. 1 (1958), 28-37.

_____. *Psychotherapy and Existentialism: Selected Papers on Logotherapy.* New York: Simon and Schuster, 1967.

_____. *The Will to Meaning: Foundations and Applications of Logotherapy.* New York: New American Library, Inc., 1969.

Friedman, Maurice, trans. *A Believing Humanism: Gleanings,* by Martin Buber. New York: Simon and Schuster, 1969.

_____. "Aiming at the Self: The Paradox of Encounter and the Human Potential Movement," *Journal of Humanistic Psychology,* 16, No. 2 (Spring, 1976), 5-34.

_____. "Dialogue and the Unique in Humanistic Psychology," *Journal of Humanistic Psychology,* 12, No. 2 (Fall, 1972), 7-22.

_____. "Existential Psychotherapy and the Image of Man," *Journal of Humanistic Psychology,* IV, No. 2 (Fall, 1964), 104-117.

_____. *The Hidden Human Image.* New York: Dell Publishing Co., Inc., 1974.

_____. *Martin Buber: The Life of Dialogue*. Chicago: University of Chicago Press, 1976.

_____. "Martin Luther King: An American Gandhi and a Modern Job," *Gandhi Marg*, XII, No. 3 (1968), 230-239.

_____, trans. *Pointing the Way: Collected Essays*, by Martin Buber. New York: Harper and Brothers, 1957.

_____. *The Problematic Rebel: Melville, Dostoievsky, Kafka, Camus*. Chicago: University of Chicago Press, 1970.

_____. *To Deny Our Nothingness: Contemporary Images of Man*. New York: Dell Publishing Co., Inc., 1967.

_____. *Touchstones of Reality: Existential Trust and the Community of Peace*. New York: E.P. Dutton and Co., Inc., 1974.

Fromm, Erich. *The Anatomy of Human Destructiveness*. Greenwich, Connecticut: Fawcett Publications, Inc. 1975.

_____. *Man for Himself: An Inquiry into the Psychology of Ethics*. Greenwich: Fawcett Publications, Inc., 1947.

_____. *The Revolution of Hope: Toward a Humanized Technology*. New York: Bantam Books, Inc., 1971.

Galtung, Johan. "Pacifism from a Sociological Point of View," *Journal of Conflict Resolution*, III, No. 1 (1959), 67-84.

Gregg, Richard B. *The Power of Nonviolence*. 2nd ed. New York: Schocken Books, 1971.

Hardy, Daphne, trans. *Darkness at Noon*, by Arthur Koestler. New York: Bantam Books, 1972.

Hodes, Aubrey. *Martin Buber: An Intimate Portrait*. New York: Viking Press, 1971.

Hope, Marjorie, and James Young. *The Struggle for Humanity: Agents of Nonviolent Change in a Violent World*. Maryknoll, N.Y: Orbis Books, 1977.

Howe, Reuel L. *The Miracle of Dialogue*. New York: The Seabury Press, 1963.

Jones, James W. "The Practice of Peoplehood," *Sojourners (May, 1977), 5-10*.

Joy, Charles R., ed. *Albert Schweitzer: An Anthology*. Boston: Beacon Press, 1967.

Keller, Paul. "A Song to Be Heard," *Messenger*, 125, No. 3 (March, 1976), 25.

King, Martin Luther. "Let Us Be Dissatisfied," *Gandhi Marg*, XII, No. 3 (1968), 218-229.

_____. "Pilgrimage to Nonviolence," *Fellowship*, (May 1976), 8-10.

Koch, Sigmond, ed. *Psychology: A Study of a Science, Volume 3, Formulations of the Person and the Social Context.* New York: McGraw Hill Book Company, Inc., 1959.

Lakey, George. *Strategy for a Living Revolution.* San Francisco: W. H. Freeman and Company, 1973.

MacGregor, G. H. C. *The New Testament Basis of Pacifism.* Nyack, New York: Fellowship, 1959.

Macky, Peter. *Violence: Right or Wrong?* Waco, Texas: Word Books, Publisher, 1973.

Marrin, Albert, ed. *War and the Christian Conscience: From Augustine to Martin Luther King, Jr.* Chicago: Henry Regnery Company, 1971.

Maslow, Abraham H. *The Farther Reaches of Human Nature.* New York: The Viking Press, 1973.

_____. *Motivation and Personality.* 2nd ed. New York: Harper and Row, Publishers, 1970.

_____, ed. *New Knowledge in Human Values.* Chicago: Henry Regnery Company, 1959.

_____. *Toward A Psychology of Being.* 2nd ed. New York: D. Van Nostrand Company, 1968.

Matson, Floyd. *The Broken Image: Man, Science, and Society.* New York: Doubleday and Company, Inc., 1966.

_____ and Ashley Montagu, ed. *The Human Dialogue: Perspectives on Communication.* New York: The Free Press, 1967.

May, Rollo. "Gregory Bateson and Humanistic Psychology," *Journal of Humanistic Psychology*, 16, No. 4 (Fall 1976), 33-51.

_____. *Man's Search for Himself.* New York: Dell Publishing Co., Inc., 1953.

_____. *Power and Innocence: A Search for the Sources of Violence.* New York: Dell Publishing Company, Inc., 1972.

Mayeroff, Milton. *On Caring.* New York: Harper and Row, Publishers, 1972.

Merton, Thomas. *Faith and Violence: Christian Teaching and Christian Practice.* Notre Dame, Indiana: University of Notre Dame Press, 1968.

_____. "The Meaning of Satyagraha," *Gandhi Marg,* X, No. 2 (1966).

_____. *Thomas Merton on Peace.* New York: McCall Publishing Company, 1971.

Miller, William Robert. *Nonviolence: A Christian Interpretation.* New York: Schocken Books, 1972.

Montagu, Ashley. *On Being Human.* New York: Hawthorn Books, Inc., 1966.

Mosbacher Eric, trans. *The Bound Man and Other Stories,* by Ilse Aichinger. New York: The Noonday Press, Inc., 1956.

Moustakas, Clark E. *Loneliness.* Englewood Cliffs, New Jersey: Prentice-Hall, Inc., 1961.

Murti, V. V. Ramana. "Buber's Dialogue and Gandhi's Satyagraha," *Journal of the History of Ideas,* 24, No. 4 (1968), 605-613.

Muste, Abraham J. *Not By Might/Christianity: The Way to Human Decency and of Holy Disobedience.* New York: Garland Publishing Inc., 1971.

_____. *Of Holy Disobedience.* Lebanon, Pennsylvania: Sowers Printing Company, 1973.

Nye, Robert D. *Conflict Among Humans: Some Basic Psychological and Social-Psychological Considerations.* New York: Springer Publishing Co., 1973.

Orwell, George. *Ninteen Eighty-four.* New York: The New American Library, Inc., 1961.

Pelton, Leroy H. *The Psychology of Nonviolence.* New York: Pergamon Press Inc., 1974.

Perls, Frederick S. *In and Out the Garbage Pail.* New York: Bantam Books., 1972.

Polanyi, Michael. *The Tacit Dimension.* New York: Doubleday and Company, Inc., 1967.

Rochlin, Gregory. *Man's Aggression: The Defense of the Self*. New York: Dell Publishing Co., Inc., 1973.

Rogers, Carl R. *Client-Centered Therapy: Its Current Practice, Implications, and Theory*. Boston: Houghton Mifflin Company, 1965.

_____. *Freedom to Learn*. Columbus: Charles E. Merrill Publishing Company, 1969.

_____ and Barry Stevens. *Person to Person: The Problem of Being Human—A New Trend in Psychology*. New York: Pocket Books, 1972.

Sappington, Roger E. *Courageous Prophet: Chapters From the Life of John Kline*. Elgin, Illinois: The Brethren Press, 1964.

Schilpp, Paul Arthur and Maurice Freidman, ed. *The Philosophy of Martin Buber*. La Salle, Illinois: Open Court Publishing Company, 1967.

Sharp, Gene. *Power and Struggle: Part One of The Politics of Nonviolent Action*. Boston: Porter Sargent Publishers, 1973.

Shull, Gordon. "The Pilgrimage of an Ex-Pacifist," *Brethren Life and Thought*, V, No. 2 (1960), 13-19.

Smith, Brewster. "On Self-Actualization: A Transambivalent Examination of a Focal Theme in Maslow's Psychology," *Journal of Humanistic Psychology*, 13, No. 2 (Spring, 1973), 17-33.

Smith, Ronald Gregor, trans. *I and Thou*, by Martin Buber. 2nd ed. New York: Charles Scribner's Sons, 1958.

Stanford, Barbara, ed. *Peacemaking: A Guide to Conflict Resolution for Individuals, Groups, and Nations*. New York: Bantam Books, Inc., 1976.

Stewart, John, ed. *Bridges Not Walls: A Book About Interpersonal Communication*. Reading, Massachusetts: Addison-Wesley Publishing Company, 1973.

Stachey, James, trans. *Civilization and Its Discontents*, by Sigmund Freud. New York: W. W. Norton and Company, Inc., 1962.

Tellis-Nayak, V. "Gandhi on the Dignity of the Human Person," *Gandhi Marg*, 7, No. 1 (1963), 40-53.

Thoreau, Henry, *On the Duty of Civil Disobedience*. London: Housmans, 1976.

Tillich, Paul. *The Courage to Be*. New Haven: Yale University Press, 1975.

Tubbs, Walter. "Beyond Perls," *Journal of Humanistic Psychology*, 12, No. 2 (Fall, 1972), 5.

Villard, Kenneth L. and Leland J. Whipple. *Beginnings in Relational Communication*. New York: John Wiley and Sons, Inc., 1976.

Walton, Richard. *Interpersonal Peacemaking: Confrontations and Third Party Consultation*. Reading Massachusetts: Addison-Wesley Publishing Co., 1969.

Watzlawick, Paul, Janet Beavin, and Don Jackson. *Pragmatics of Human Communication: A Study of Interactional Patterns, Pathologies, and Paradoxes*. New York; W. W. Norton and Company, Inc., 1967.

_____, John H. Weakland, and Richard Fisch. *Change: Principles of Problem Formation and Problem Resolution*. New York: W. W. Norton and Company, Inc., 1974.

Weiss, Richard. *The American Myth of Success: From Horatio Alger to Norman Vincent Peale*. New York: New York Basic Books, Inc., Publishers, 1969.

Wilson, Marjorie Kerr, trans. *Civilized Man's Eight Deadly Sins*, by Konrad Lorenz. New York: Harcourt Brace Jovanovich, Inc., 1974.

_____, trans. *On Aggression*, by Konrad Lorenz. New York: Harcourt, Brace and Wilson, Inc., 1966.

Yoder, John Howard. *The Politics of Jesus*. Grand Rapids: William B. Eerdmans Publishing Company, 1972.

Zunkel, C. Wayne. "Violence and Nonviolence," *Six Papers on Peace: A Symposium*. Elgin: Church of the Brethren General Board, 1969.